THE CATHOLIC CASE AGAINST WAR

THE CATHOLIC CASE AGAINST WAR

A BRIEF GUIDE

DAVID CARROLL COCHRAN

University of Notre Dame Press
Notre Dame, Indiana

Copyright © 2024 by the University of Notre Dame

University of Notre Dame Press
Notre Dame, Indiana 46556
undpress.nd.edu

All Rights Reserved

Published in the United States of America

Library of Congress Control Number: 2023946555

ISBN: 978-0-268-20787-8 (Hardback)
ISBN: 978-0-268-20789-2 (Paperback)
ISBN: 978-0-268-20786-1 (WebPDF)
ISBN: 978-0-268-20790-8 (Epub3)

For Stephen and Brian

*We need to reject war, a place of death
where fathers and mothers bury their children,
where men kill their brothers and sisters
without even having seen them,
where the powerful decide and the poor die.*

—Pope Francis, *Angelus*, March 27, 2022

CONTENTS

Acknowledgments ix

Introduction 1

CHAPTER 1
War's Death, Destruction, and Dehumanization 7

CHAPTER 2
War's False Promises and the Power of Nonviolence 27

CHAPTER 3
Preventing War through Greater Global Governance 51

CHAPTER 4
Preventing War through Economic and Political Justice 75

CHAPTER 5
Abolishing War 101

Recommended Reading 125

Notes 127

Works Cited 149

Index 177

ACKNOWLEDGMENTS

Thanks to my wonderful family, to many great friends and colleagues at Loras College, to students in POL 321: War and Pacifism over the years, to participants in the Catholic Nonviolence Initiative and its ongoing discussion groups, and to members of the Dubuque International Day of Peace planning committee. For their guidance and suggestions, thanks as well to Emily King, Matt Dowd, Steffi Marchman, Wendy McMillen, and everyone at the University of Notre Dame Press, to Bob Banning at Turning Leaves Editorial, and to the manuscript's three reviewers. Finally, I am grateful for research support from Loras College's annual John Cardinal O'Connor Chair for Catholic Thought, its summer Ahlgren Research Grants, and its fantastic library staff.

INTRODUCTION

"Never again war!" It has become a mantra for popes over the last five decades, one signaling the emergence of Catholic teaching as a remarkably powerful voice against warfare in the contemporary world.[1] The church's case against war combines a sweeping critique of war's nature and a detailed vision for abolishing it by strengthening its alternatives and actively building peace. This case amounts to, in the words of John Paul II, a comprehensive and urgent "No to War!"[2]

The church has not always been such a strong critic of war. Although the earliest Christians usually rejected participation in warfare as contrary to the gospel, starting in the fourth century thinkers such as Ambrose and Augustine gradually laid the foundations of the Christian just war tradition. Developed over the centuries since, this tradition argues that war, while often terrible, is sometimes necessary to protect a just and peaceful order given the realities of sin in the world. Under certain conditions—a just cause, right intention, last resort, and others—going to war is morally legitimate. And fighting such wars once underway can be morally just too, as long as participants observe certain moral limits—not intentionally attacking civilians, avoiding disproportionate destruction, treating prisoners humanely, and others. This was the dominant lens the Catholic Church used to analyze war for most of its history up into the twentieth century. Not all wars are just, but some are, and war itself, while regrettable, is a normal and often legitimate part of the way countries behave in the world.[3]

Beginning in the twentieth century, however, Catholic teaching on war and peace underwent significant shifts, especially after Vatican II's promise to "undertake an evaluation of war with an entirely new attitude."[4] While its interpretation of the just war tradition was once flexible enough to accommodate war as a normal part of statecraft, the Vatican increasingly applied stricter interpretations, using them to condemn wars for such things as lacking just cause or right intention, ignoring alternatives demanded by the last resort requirement, unleashing disproportionate destruction on societies, and, especially, indiscriminately killing civilians. Rather than emphasizing war's necessity in protecting a just and peaceful order, Catholic teaching's emerging case against war condemned it as a threat to such an order, creating cycles of violence, devastation, and oppression that only made things worse. Alongside these growing condemnations of war and, eventually, calls to abolish it completely, the church emphasized alternatives to armed conflict such as negotiation, mediation, and nonviolent resistance. It urged the world to address the roots of war through greater global cooperation, international law, and a commitment to sustainable economic development, human rights, and democratic political institutions.[5] In this way, the Vatican increasingly emphasized principles associated with what is often now called a "just peace" perspective.[6]

While this shift to a much more critical view of war has been dramatic, there remains the question of whether Catholic teaching still allows any space for a just war under certain conditions. On the yes side, even as Vatican statements increasingly condemned war, they allowed for narrow exceptions as a last resort—either in national self-defense or as military interventions to prevent humanitarian disasters such as genocide—at least until humanity succeeds in ending war itself. Vatican II's *Gaudium et Spes* states: "As long as the danger of war remains and there is no competent and sufficiently powerful authority at the international level, governments cannot be denied the right to legitimate defense once every means of peaceful settlement has been exhausted." And John Paul II, who once said "we are not pacifists," gives a qualified endorsement to "humanitarian interventions" to disarm an "unjust aggressor" when other means to prevent grave abuse of innocent populations have failed.[7]

More recently, however, church teaching may have closed this remaining space for morally permitted war. While pointing to the need to resist "unjust aggression," Francis states, "I don't say bomb, make war," and calls the decision "to engage in war" a "mistaken understanding of our own principles." In 2020's *Fratelli Tutti*, Francis warns, "War can easily be chosen by invoking all sorts of allegedly humanitarian, defensive or precautionary excuses. . . . In recent decades, every single war has been ostensibly 'justified.'" The nature of modern warfare makes it "very difficult" to ever satisfy traditional just war criteria and therefore to even "speak of the possibility of a 'just war'" today. According to Francis, Augustine "forged a concept of 'just war' that we no longer uphold in our own day."[8] And in statements addressing the war following Russia's 2022 invasion of Ukraine, Francis is even more direct, saying "wars are always unjust" and "there is no such thing as a just war: they do not exist!"[9]

There have, then, been major and, given the church's millennia-long existence, relatively recent developments in Catholic teaching on war and peace over the last century, ones rooted in shifts in both how the church views the world and how it communicates the nonviolent teachings of Jesus in the Gospels. And these developments are ongoing. This means it is an area of teaching that is still relatively fluid, and therefore one necessarily marked by a number of ambiguities and unanswered questions, especially around if and when armed force is ever morally permitted. Until we have a major authoritative document, such as a papal encyclical, that directly addresses the question in detail, those who believe Catholic teaching permits some instances of armed force, either in self-defense or to protect vulnerable populations from mass atrocities such as genocide, can certainly find support for their position, just as those who believe the church no longer permits such force can find support for theirs.

This issue of if and when contemporary church teaching permits any resort to war is important, and it has rightly sparked a rich dialogue among Catholic ethicists and theologians.[10] It is crucial to realize, however, that the issue of narrow exceptions in Catholic teaching that may or may not allow military force should not obscure the much larger, systematic, and comprehensive case against *war itself* that the church has developed over the last century. That case is this book's focus.

— Unfortunately, the Catholic case against war is underappreciated for two reasons. First, many people, Catholic and not, don't know enough about it. Like other areas of Catholic social teaching, what the church says about war and peace still doesn't get enough attention from the pulpit, the press, and political discourse. It doesn't help that while the Vatican has much to say on the topic, it is scattered across decades of different encyclicals, statements, and messages. This book's first purpose, then, is to draw on these texts to gather in one, accessible place the essential features of Catholic teaching's case against war, one useful for those who want to know more about it and who can share it with others.

While many Catholic thinkers, activists, and national bishops' conferences have made significant contributions to developing Catholic teaching in this area, I have decided, in the interest of a more concise and focused account, to only use formal Vatican documents and papal statements. It is important to note that the church does not consider all of these equally authoritative; an encyclical carries more weight than a homily or press interview. But together they constitute the clearest articulation of what those officially charged with communicating church teaching have to say about war and peace. For ease of reference, I have listed these documents and statements separately in the works cited section at the book's end.

The second, and more troubling, reason the Catholic case against war is underappreciated is that, even among those familiar with it, too many consider it unrealistic. Critics frequently dismiss it as hopelessly naïve, sentimental, and utopian, while even those sympathetic to its moral witness can worry that it is too optimistic for how the world really works.[11] So the book's second, and more important, purpose is to demonstrate how thoroughly realistic the church's case against war really is.

There is a large and sophisticated body of empirical and historical research about war. Those who study armed conflict have learned much about its nature, its causes, its alternatives, and ways to prevent it in the first place. By drawing on key findings from this work, I detail just how consistent the Catholic case is with what we actually know about the realities of war and peace.[12]

The Catholic Church's case against war turns out to not only be morally inspiring but also empirically sound. It is among the most comprehensive, powerful, and, yes, deeply realistic takes on war and peace in the world today.

CHAPTER 1

WAR'S DEATH, DESTRUCTION, AND DEHUMANIZATION

Given how central "the sacredness and inviolability of human life" is in contemporary Catholic teaching, the mass killing inherent in war is unsurprisingly front-and-center in the church's case against it. War is a key part of the larger "culture of death" that church teaching condemns. In the words of John Paul II, "War itself is an attack on human life."[1]

Of particular concern is the scale of killing and its many innocent victims. Writing just a few months into World War I, Benedict XV laments in *Ad Beatissimi Apostolorum*: "There is no limit to the measure of ruin and of slaughter; day by day the earth is drenched with newly-shed blood, and is covered with the bodies of the wounded and the slain." Paul VI decries war's "useless massacres" resulting in the "blood of millions," and John Paul II denounces war for its "millions and millions of victims" and for how it "destroys the lives of innocent people."[2] While church teaching does count soldiers caught up in conflicts not of their own making among war's victims, as when Francis mourns the death of both Ukrainian and Russian soldiers in their war that began in 2022, it more often focuses on the shocking numbers of noncombatant deaths during war, condemning "civilian populations torn apart" and how dead civilians are casually dismissed as "collateral damage."[3] And it regularly highlights the exceptional horror of so many children killed. As John Paul II writes, "Sadly, many of the world's children are innocent victims of war. In recent years millions of them have been wounded or killed; a veritable slaughter."[4]

Over the last century, the Vatican has been particularly alarmed by how the technology of war, including weapons of mass destruction, can magnify the potential scale and indiscriminate nature of its killing. It denounces the "terrifying destructive force of modern weapons," the way they pave the way for "a savagery far surpassing that of the past," and how they "have granted war an uncontrollable destructive power over great numbers of innocent civilians."[5] Indeed, Francis has made clear that Catholic teaching considers a country's even possessing nuclear weapons deeply immoral.[6]

— Of course, recognizing war's killing is nothing new. For traditional just war thinkers such as Augustine, it may be regrettable, but sometimes war is nonetheless necessary to protect what he called "the tranquility of order," meaning a humane, secure, lawful society where people can live their lives free of violence and abuse.[7] The Vatican continues to emphasize the importance of such an order today. It regularly uses phrases such as "well-ordered" institutions, "civic order," and "tranquil social coexistence" to indicate societies that promote human flourishing by being rooted in security, cooperation, justice, and human dignity.[8]

But whereas Augustine and church teaching in the past may have considered war necessary to protect the tranquility of order, the Vatican is now far more likely to condemn war as actually destroying it. A just order based on violence is neither just nor orderly, and it certainly isn't tranquil. In *Pacem in Terris*, John XXIII writes, "There is nothing human about a society that is welded together by force," and Francis adds, "We cannot claim to maintain stability in the world through fear of annihilation."[9] Those who try to protect a just and peaceful order through violence, domination, threats, intimidation, or a balance of military power betray the very thing they claim to protect; war is not a guarantor of just order, but is itself a form of injustice and disorder.[10] The Second Vatican Council contrasts war's "ravages" with a "more genuinely human" order, and Francis condemns the world's "wars and conflicts that bring only death and destruction in their wake."[11] Indeed, a crucial part of the Catholic case against war is calling attention to the long train of suffering and destruction that it produces. War doesn't only kill people; it devastates a humane social order even for those it leaves alive.[12]

A passage from Francis in his 2021 World Day of Peace message illustrates this sweeping critique:

> Tragically, many regions and communities can no longer remember a time when they dwelt in security and peace. Numerous cities have become epicentres of insecurity: citizens struggle to maintain their normal routine in the face of indiscriminate attacks by explosives, artillery and small arms. Children are unable to study. Men and women cannot work to support their families. Famine is spreading in places where it was previously unknown. People are being forced to take flight, leaving behind not only their homes but also their family history and their cultural roots.[13]

Similarly, John Paul II laments "families and countries destroyed, an ocean of refugees, misery, hunger, disease, underdevelopment and the loss of immense resources."[14]

Vatican statements on this theme often include images of physical, cultural, and environmental wreckage left by war. Paul VI invokes "frightening ruins," John Paul II speaks of the "disintegration of human relations and the irreparable loss of an immense artistic and environmental patrimony," and Francis deplores the "grave harm to the environment and the cultural riches of people."[15]

An area of particular concern is war's impact on children, the family, and the home. John Paul II calls the family an institution that is key to an "enduring peaceful order," and church teaching condemns how war devastates it and the lives of its members. It emphasizes the intense suffering of orphans, widows, child soldiers, refugees, and victims of sexual abuse, forced labor, disease, or famine caused by war.[16] Francis is especially powerful in condemning this dimension of armed conflict. He states, "One out of every six children in our world is affected by the violence of war and its effects, even when they are not enrolled as child soldiers or held hostage by armed groups." He laments all the "wounded children, maimed children, orphaned children, children who have the remnants of war as toys, children who do not know how to smile," as well as "mothers who lost their children, and the boys and girls maimed or deprived of their childhood." And, pointing to how "armed conflicts and other forms of organized violence continue to trigger the movement of peoples within national borders and beyond," Francis writes, "In a spirit of compassion, let us embrace all those fleeing from war and hunger."[17]

In highlighting these types of intense suffering brought by war, church teaching also emphasizes the deep and lasting wounds for persons and communities over time. War creates legacies of damage and pain that, according to John Paul II, "remain long unhealed." In *Fratelli Tutti*, Francis invokes this ongoing suffering among war's survivors, arguing that in listening to their stories, "we will be able to grasp the abyss of evil at the heart of war." Francis demands that we recognize the true impact of choosing war: "This means destroying the future, causing dramatic trauma in the lives of the smallest and most innocent among us. This is the brutality of war—a barbaric and sacrilegious act!"[18]

Another dimension of war's destructiveness that church teaching frequently denounces is its economic costs. Not only does war disproportionately afflict the poor and vulnerable, but warfare itself causes more poverty.[19] Here is Benedict XV during World War I again: "Trade is at a standstill; agriculture is abandoned; the arts are reduced to inactivity; the wealthy are in difficulties; the poor are reduced to abject misery; all are in distress."[20] And here is John Paul II eight decades later: "War worsens the sufferings of the poor; indeed, it creates new poor by destroying means of subsistence, homes and property, and by eating away at the very fabric of the social environment. Young people see their hopes for the future shattered and too often, as victims, they become irresponsible agents of conflict."[21]

Poverty and the material suffering of the vulnerable are also made worse by the resources poured into preparing for and fighting wars. Again and again, Vatican documents decry the way governments— driven by fear, militarism, and the interests of the arms industry—spend vast sums on weapons rather than economic development, healthcare, education, and other forms of human welfare.[22] In *Mater et Magistra*, John XXIII denounces this "vast expenditure of human energy and natural resources on projects that are disruptive of human society rather than beneficial to it." The 1971 World Synod of Catholic Bishops at the Vatican protests: "The arms race is a threat to our highest good, which is life; it makes poor peoples and individuals yet more miserable, while making richer the already powerful." John Paul II calls arms races "insane" since resources "are used for weapons rather than for development, peace and justice." And Paul VI is most blunt, calling military spending "an act of theft" and an "act of aggression" against the world's most vulnerable, one that is "starving the poor to death" for lack of resources.[23]

Finally, the Catholic case that war destroys rather than protects the "tranquility of order" includes war's dehumanization and how it corrodes the very virtues that a just and humane society requires. For John Paul II, war is fundamentally "inhuman" and "always a defeat for humanity." It "teaches how to kill, throws into upheaval even the lives of those who do the killing and leaves behind a trail of resentment and hatred."[24] Francis reinforces this theme of dehumanization, condemning war for lowering persons "to the status of objects." It is rooted in and cultivates a profound "indifference to others and their dignity" that destroys the very "moral and spiritual integrity" of persons and communities.

He sums up the church's view of war thus: "Every war is a form of fratricide that destroys the human family's innate vocation to brotherhood."[25]

DEATH

In their detailed studies of war's nature, the historian Joanna Bourke and military psychologist Dave Grossman both arrive at the same conclusion: once you strip away the historical causes and moral justifications, war's inescapable essence is its killing. For Bourke, it is "the characteristic act" of war, and Grossman states that "killing is what war is all about."[26] Describing their experience of combat, many soldiers agree. In his autobiography, U.S. Navy sniper Chris Kyle writes, "My job was killing," and Ken Lukowiak, who fought in the British Army during the Falklands War, recalls: "We were professional soldiers, and that's what professional soldiers do—kill people."[27]

And war is not merely killing, but killing at scale—the massive, organized, sustained slaughter of fellow human beings. Scroll through any online tabulation of estimated deaths per war across history, and the sheer numbers of people killed quickly become mind-numbing. It's not just the cases we may know best—the hundreds of thousands who perished in the American Civil War, the tens of millions killed in World War I or World War II, or the third of Europe's German-speaking population that died in the Thirty Years War. Eighth-century China's An Lushan Revolt killed an estimated thirty-six million people, around a sixth of the world's population at the time. The Spanish Civil War killed a half-million people, as did the U.S. seizure of the Philippines from Spain in the early twentieth century. Nine million people died in the Russian Civil War. Between one and two million people died during Bangladesh's independence war against Pakistan, about the same as in Afghanistan following the Soviet invasion. And the War of the Triple Alliance, fought in Paraguay in the late 1860s, killed over half that country's entire population.[28] The list could go on for the rest of this chapter. As Catholic teaching emphasizes, warfare is an ongoing mass assault on human life.

— Among all these persons killed by war throughout human history, the majority are its innocent victims. The most obvious are civilian noncombatants, whose deaths contemporary Vatican statements so frequently condemn. While some civilians may be guilty of supporting or profiting from wars of aggression or repression, almost all noncombatants caught up in wars are not responsible for starting them, do not participate in their killing, and seek only to avoid their violence. As Erasmus observed five centuries ago, "Princes wage war unscathed and their generals thrive on it, while the main flood of misfortune sweeps over the peasants and humble citizens, who have no interest in war and gave no occasion for it."[29] Yet killing such noncombatants is inseparable from warfare and always has been. Dead civilians are so common and widespread in war that scholars trying to gather accurate casualty estimates for even recent conflicts struggle to do so given the sheer volume.[30]

Sometimes killing civilians is intentional. This can be deliberate strategy — from ancient warriors' putting entire towns to the sword to strategic bombing in World War II that purposely targeted civilian populations — or it can be soldiers' killing civilians for sport, an age-old practice that still flourishes today.[31] Inuit oral traditions describe the ancient practice of raids on rival communities where the goal was to "eliminate everyone in the village one by one, going from house to house and killing them while they slept."[32] On a larger scale, the 1631 sack of Magdeburg, Germany, saw thirty thousand residents slaughtered.[33] Winston Churchill, as secretary of state for war in 1920, justified using chemical weapons against civilians to put down rebellions against British colonial rule, saying, "I am strongly in favor of using poison gas against uncivilized tribes."[34] In a letter to his wife, a German soldier describes killing Jewish children in Belarus during World War II: "Infants flew in great arcs through the air, and we shot them to pieces in flight."[35] One participant in the My Lai massacre, where American soldiers killed almost five hundred noncombatants, mainly women and children, recalls: "We were told to leave nothing standing. We did what we were told, regardless of whether they were civilians."[36] In 1998, the Taliban in Afghanistan sacked the town of Mazar-e-Sharif, spending several days torturing and killing its inhabitants, many by being locked into shipping containers to be slowly "baked alive in the desert sun."[37] These examples illustrate the conclusion Steven LeBlanc and Katherine Register draw, in their study of war's origins, that "the act of massacring civilians is as ancient as war itself," and John Keegan's observation, in his influential *A History of Warfare*, that targeting civilian populations has been "standard practice" from war's beginnings to today.[38]

Sometimes killing noncombatants is not so much deliberate as merely indiscriminate. In such cases, warriors may not seek out civilians to kill specifically, but they also don't bother to distinguish them from combatants either. As the popular saying dismissively puts it: "Kill them all and let God sort them out." The history of warfare is marked by siege and blockade tactics that use hunger and disease against combatants and noncombatant alike.[39] And indiscriminately shelling areas from a distance similarly kills both. Some kinds of modern weapons are also particularly indiscriminate (as we have seen, the Vatican is especially likely to condemn these types of arms). Most obvious are weapons of mass destruction such as nuclear or biological ones. But other armaments, such as landmines and cluster munitions, also end up killing far more noncombatants than soldiers. Unexploded landmines from the Vietnam War still regularly kill civilians fifty years after its end; children are especially at risk of death in places such as Iraq, Afghanistan, and Ukraine from picking up unexploded cluster bomblets; and environmental contaminants that remain decades after wars end continue to threaten the lives of local populations around the world.[40]

The traditional rules of war, now enshrined in treaties such as the Geneva Conventions, include prohibitions on intentionally or indiscriminately killing civilians. Wars in which one or both parties attempt in good faith to follow such rules have been the exception in human history; either the rules didn't exist at the time, they were simply ignored, or parties paid them lip service while continuing to engage in indiscriminate killing in the name of military necessity.[41] But even when belligerents do try to uphold rules designed to protect noncombatants in war, as many professionalized militaries do today, they can end up killing enormous numbers of civilians anyway.

The explanation lies in the nature of warfare itself. It takes place in an environment of violence and uncertainty. Under often brutal conditions, heightened fear, and a culture of aggression, soldiers wield highly lethal weapons and use them as a matter of course. It is a context with a unique and remarkably low threshold for killing.[42] Actual combat often features what Grossman calls "gray-area killings," where soldiers are unsure of the precise status or actual threat posed by people they are killing.[43] The circumstances of danger and the need for "force protection" encourage soldiers not to take chances by holding their fire, which shifts significant risk to civilians caught in warzones. As one American soldier in Iraq commented when responding to civilians mistakenly killed at checkpoints, "We didn't know what was in that bus. . . . I'd rather see more of them dead than any of my friends."[44] Another factor is the reality of target selection in modern war. Combatants often fire weapons—from small arms to artillery to missiles—at people based not on who they are as individuals but instead on broader categories such as location, being a fighting-age male, or behavior that might be suspicious but could also be innocuous (is the person on drone surveillance planting a roadside bomb or repairing an irrigation pipe?).[45] In any complex situation marked by pressure and rapid decision-making, mistakes are inevitable. And even when soldiers do fire at actual enemy combatants, spillover from their powerful weapons often kills nearby noncombatants as well.[46] Is it any wonder so many civilians end up dead in wars?

Now also consider that all of this doesn't yet account for the many noncombatants killed not directly by war's weapons but rather by the famine, disease, and exposure it brings in its wake. When armed conflict destroys crops, livestock, water treatment plants, power grids, hospitals, transportation systems, and homes, death rates among local populations soar, especially among children, the elderly, and the sick. As Hugo Slim remarks in his study of noncombatants in war, when it comes to civilian casualties, "most people die *from war* rather than *in battle*."[47]

There is a common misperception, one that also appears in some Vatican statements, that modern weapons have made war more indiscriminate overall, killing a greater percentage of civilians compared to wars of the past. Technology has made modern weapons far more powerful and destructive, killing enormous numbers of people, but it doesn't seem to have decisively changed the ratio of noncombatant to combatant deaths. This is not because modern warfare doesn't kill lots of civilians, but rather because war has always done so. Set-piece battles between soldiers lined up in fields far from civilians, which many people imagine when picturing wars in earlier ages, did happen, but they were the exception, and they usually took place within larger wars with plenty of civilian killing.[48] You don't need modern technology for mass destruction. As Robert Holmes says of the Roman sack of Carthage in 146 BCE, "The Romans annihilated the Carthaginians in the third Punic War as effectively as if they had dropped a nuclear bomb on them."[49] According to Joshua Goldstein, while the civilian percentage of war deaths compared to soldiers can vary widely depending on the particular conflict, the average across human history is roughly 50 percent.[50] Killing civilians, then, is not some kind of unfortunate exception more likely in modern warfare. Equaling combatant deaths throughout war's existence, it is clearly a feature, not a bug.

— There is a powerful tendency to react to noncombatant deaths in war differently depending on their side of a conflict. While belligerents usually publicize and lament dead civilians from their group, often invoking them to bolster the righteousness of their cause, they usually rationalize or ignore an opponent's civilian deaths. As the war correspondent Chris Hedges puts it, "While we venerate and mourn our own dead we are curiously indifferent about those we kill. . . . Our dead matter, theirs do not."[51] Public opinion research backs this up. In *The Deaths of Others*, John Tirman details just how uninterested and unsympathetic the American public historically is to civilian war deaths among foreign populations. Even when public opinion turns against participation in a conflict, as in the case of the Vietnam War, it is due to ongoing casualties among American soldiers rather than non-American civilian deaths.[52] There is also evidence that as nationalist and ethnocentric attitudes increase, so too does indifference to noncombatant fatalities on the opponent's side.[53]

There are some typical ways to justify, minimize, or disregard civilian deaths on the other side of a war.[54] One is refusing to even recognize the difference between soldiers and civilians, viewing everyone on the enemy side as collectively guilty or threatening, especially as wars descend into cycles of reprisals and revenge. As an American officer said of bombing Japanese cities, "There are no civilians in Japan," or as an Algerian Islamist insurgent said, "With the exception of those who are with us, all others are apostates and deserve to die."[55] Another way is with the equivalent of a dismissive shrug. Waving away noncombatant deaths with some variation of the phrase "that's war" is remarkably common, from President George W. Bush during the post-9/11 war on terror, to terrorists who targeted civilians in bombings in Israel and London, to Lt. William Calley on his role in the My Lai massacre.[56] A more sophisticated way is to hide behind semantic evasions. As long as all those dead civilians were not technically "intended" but were merely "collateral damage," then it is possible to safely ignore them (even if they themselves would likely have protested against such moral reasoning if anyone had bothered to ask them).[57]

Of course, being realistic about war means fully facing the reality of its noncombatant fatalities on all sides. This is what the Vatican's case against war does. It identifies killing innocent civilians as an inescapable feature of war itself, condemning their staggering death toll and recognizing each of them as equally a victim regardless of what national, ethnic, religious, or other groups they belong to.

— Catholic teaching includes soldiers among war's victims too, though not as frequently or powerfully as it condemns civilian deaths. This is important because most soldiers are also innocent in important ways. That may sound odd, since as active participants in war's killing, soldiers are considered legitimate targets in war (unless they are wounded, surrendering, or similarly out of combat). But like most civilians, most soldiers are not responsible for the war itself. They may be reluctant participants or even forced to participate. In many wars the majority of soldiers killed on both sides have been drafted to fight, and some scholars estimate that the majority of armed conflicts in the world today include coerced child soldiers.[58] Most soldiers are caught up in wars not of their making and are just trying to survive. In the words of Erasmus, "They must either slay without mercy, or fall without pity."[59] Accounts offered by soldiers themselves often echo this. A US Marine in World War II, after killing a Japanese soldier and finding a photo of the dead man's family in his wallet, recalled thinking, "What the hell am I doing here? Here's a guy that's never done a thing to me, and yet I had to kill him because his boss said 'go to war' and my boss said 'go to war.'"[60]

The rules of war themselves actually acknowledge this type of innocence among ordinary soldiers. Why do the rules prohibit killing soldiers when wounded or surrendering, or mistreating them when taken prisoner, or punishing rather than releasing them once the war is over? Because as long as such soldiers have themselves followed the rules of war, they have done nothing wrong. Unlike criminals, they don't deserve punishment.[61] And this is true even if they are fighting in a war of aggression or repression. The Catholic Church itself has a prime example in its own Pope Benedict XVI, who was conscripted as a teenager into the German military during World War II, was captured by Allied troops as Hitler's regime collapsed, spent about a month in a POW camp, and was released without punishment to live the rest of his life following a vocation that led him to the papacy.[62]

Notice, however, that the very soldiers the rules of war deem immune from killing or lesser punishments once they are out of the war, because they haven't done anything to deserve it, are also, according to the same rules, free game for slaughter during the war, and not just during actual combat, but also when they are miles away sitting scared in a trench, asleep in their bunk, or seasick on a transport ship. Indeed, as military experts often note, the deadliest time for soldiers in warfare is when their lines have broken and they are in full retreat fleeing for their lives.[63] At the end of the First Gulf War, for instance, the US military strafed defenseless retreating Iraqi troops from the air, killing thousands of them along the notorious "highway of death."[64]

As with civilian deaths, the sheer scale at which war slaughters soldiers can be overwhelming. At the 1571 naval Battle of Lepanto, 30,000 combatants drowned in a single day. By the end of the eighteenth century's Seven Years' War, the Prussian army had seen 180,000 of its soldiers killed, three times as many as it started the war with. During World War I, tens of thousands of Ottoman soldiers froze to death in just one operation against Russian troops, and over 700,000 soldiers died during the battle for Verdun. Just a few decades later, during its World War II invasion of the Soviet Union, the German army killed 4,000,000 Soviet soldiers in the first six months alone.[65] This slaughter of soldiers is another reason why any clear-eyed scrutiny of war's nature must put mass killing at its core.

DESTRUCTION AND DEHUMANIZATION

In early Mesoamerican writing, the symbol for war was a burning building.[66] There is good reason for the frequent connection between warfare and images of destruction. As Keegan shows in his history of the institution, "Laying waste the enemy's land" has been part of war from its very beginning.[67] Centuries ago, Erasmus condemned the "train of evils" that mean "war always brings about the wreck of everything that is good, and the tide of war overflows with everything that is worst."[68] Christopher Blattman, a contemporary scholar of armed conflict, is even more blunt: "War is ruinous."[69] Catholic teaching is correct when it emphasizes that in addition to its mass killing, war devastates communities, sabotages a humane social order, and unleashes intense human suffering.

Those who study war provide a grim catalog of these impacts.[70] War causes spikes in famine, contaminated drinking water, communicable disease, and birth defects. It destroys homes and infrastructure, producing staggering numbers of refugees struggling to live in brutal and dangerous conditions. Gangs and organized crime thrive in war zones. War drives surges in looting, arson, drug trafficking, assault, rape, torture and mutilation, terrorism, and the desecration of holy sites and objects. Enslavement and other forms of coerced and trafficked labor are common, whether as fighters, porters, sex workers, or builders of fortifications. So too are detention, restricted movement, and suppression of liberties such as speech, the press, and religious exercise. War creates pervasive fear and collapses social trust. It sets back gross domestic product (GDP) and trade levels by decades, pushes large portions of the population into poverty, and diverts money from human needs to militaries and warlords. The technology of modern armed conflict in particular can leave a trail of environmental destruction and toxic pollution for decades. War leaves children without parents, parents without children, and spouses, lovers, and friends without each other. It is no wonder that many who survive war, soldiers and civilians, live the rest of their lives with deep physical and emotional wounds — it brings an aftermath of chronic pain, limited mobility, post-traumatic stress disorder, guilt, despair, fear, humiliation, and rage. Most heartbreaking are the legacies of suffering born by children, such as the teenage girl haunted by memories of seeing her neighbors die screaming with their feet stuck in melting asphalt during the firebombing of Hamburg during World War II, or the note left at the Vietnam Veterans Memorial in Washington, DC, that read, "I have dreamed of the day you'll come home and finally be my dad."[71]

— Each item on the list above contains worlds of cruelty and pain all its own. It is worth taking a closer look at just one of them to illustrate. Sixteen centuries ago, Augustine called rape an "ancient and customary evil" of war.[72] He was correct then and still is today; rape is inseparable from the institution of war.[73] Nothing documents this better than Christina Lamb's *Our Bodies, Their Battlefields*, her examination of the pervasiveness of rape in warfare, both historically and today, and the devastating consequences this has for its victims, overwhelmingly women and girls (though sometimes men and boys too).[74]

From Herodotus in the fifth century BCE, who described Phoenician women "raped successively by so many Persian soldiers that they died," to the two million German women raped by Soviet soldiers in the final stages of World War II (as word of the rampages spread, hundreds of thousands of women and girls took their own lives as soldiers approached their homes), to the standard two hours Franco's Spanish Civil War officers gave troops to rape and mutilate women in towns they captured, to the mass rape committed by Turkish troops in their 1974 invasion of Cyprus, where girls who reported to Turkish officers that they had been raped were raped again by those same officers, to a single hospital in the Democratic Republic of Congo that has treated over fifty-five thousand women and girls for injuries from rape over the last two decades of civil war, Lamb makes it clear that rape has always been "a systematic weapon of war" and that still today in many war zones "it is more dangerous to be a woman" than a man.[75]

The book details how warfare commonly involves victims being held in sexual slavery in camps, to be raped dozens of times a day; being publicly gang raped, with family members and neighbors forced to watch; seeing family members killed before being raped; and having sexual organs mutilated as part of rapes. A Filipino woman named Lola Narcisa Claveria remembers being enslaved by Japanese soldiers during World War II along with her sisters after seeing their family members killed and house burned, saying, "Almost every night we were being raped, sometimes by two or three soldiers, and in front of the others. . . . They raped me over and over and burnt us with cigarettes. . . . Every day I would pray that night would not come and the sun would not go down because then the Japanese would rape us." Jane Mukunizwa, a Congolese woman, recalls being raped at fourteen years old by Interahamwe fighters: "We were tied to trees with our arms out as if we were being crucified. It was as if we had already died." And a Rohingya mother named Munira describes what happened when Burmese soldiers attacked her village, killed all the men, and raped the women and girls: "I was raped by five men. . . . I saw two girls dead near me. . . . By the time the sun came up I was barely conscious. . . . I couldn't walk but only crawl. . . . I tried to find my children. Then I saw a small boy lying face down, shot in the back. It was Subat Alam, my eldest. He had been running towards me. He was eight."[76]

Lamb's accounts show how those raped in war are "double victims," since the aftermath of physical injuries, psychological wounds, shame, social ostracism, and suicide can amount to "slow murder."[77] After being abducted by a Serbian paramilitary member to be gang raped, a Kosovar woman named Vasfije Krasniqi-Goodman says, "I begged him to kill me but he said no, you'll suffer more this way. . . . The man was right I would suffer more. Every day my mind goes to what happened." During the Bangladesh independence war in 1971, Hanzera Khatam recalls how after a group of Pakistani soldiers caught her, stomped her three-year-old daughter to death, and "raped me so much I lost consciousness," she made her way home, but "the villagers wouldn't let me back in the village."[78] The terrible aftermath of being raped in war is compounded by the impunity attackers often enjoy. Many victims have to see their rapists walking around communities free. Whey they speak out, they are frequently ignored or blamed by authorities; a common taunt is that they are not attractive enough to rape.

Dismissing wartime rape goes beyond individual victims to the very practice itself. Lamb details the history of rape's being "trivialized and regarded as acceptable when it occurred in war," with "military and political leaders shrugging it off as if it were a sideshow" or denying it happened at all.[79] Since it is "the world's most neglected war crime," she writes, "you won't find these women's names in the history books or on the war memorials we pass in our railway stations or town centers."[80] She demonstrates how in the aftermath of wars from Guatemala to Germany to the Philippines to Bangladesh to Serbia, mass rape that occurs in wars gets erased in such things as treaty negotiations, school textbooks, or public monuments to the war's victims.[81]

— As normalized mass rape exemplifies, war unleashes dehumanizing brutality of a unique kind and on a vast scale. Those who observe or experience war frequently describe a world of inverted morality. Saint Cyprian said of war in the third century: "Murder, considered a crime when people commit it singly, is transformed into a virtue when they do it en masse." And Hedges echoes this today when he describes war as the "collapse of a moral universe, a world where right and wrong have been turned upside down," where "perversion may become moral, guilt may become honor, and the gunning down of unarmed people, including children, may be defined as heroic."[82] An Irish veteran of World War I recalled: "You do such things and get praise for them, such as smashing a fellow's skull, or putting a bullet through him, which if you were to do at home you'd soon be on the run, with a hue and cry and all the police of the country at your heels."[83] After World War II, the chief American counsel at the Nuremberg Tribunals commented: "War consists largely of acts that would be criminal if performed in the time of peace—killing, wounding, kidnapping, destroying or carrying off other people's property. Such conduct is not regarded as criminal if it takes place in the course of war." Participant accounts from that same war confirm this view. The American William Manchester described killing a Japanese soldier as "a betrayal of what I'd been taught since a child," where "murder is the most heinous of crimes," and a German soldier explained war's mass violence by saying, "This is no kindergarten."[84]

This is actually a real challenge for militaries. To get ordinary people to fight in wars and do things normally thought deeply wrong, it is often necessary, as Gwynne Dyer puts it, to "reverse the moral training of a lifetime."[85] Turning people into effective warriors, whether it is in professionalized armies or irregular militias, requires a particular kind of dehumanizing conditioning.[86] Grossman details this process in his book *On Killing*. Most people have a deep inner reluctance to kill, one rooted in an awareness of common humanity, which is why doing so often comes at such a high psychological cost, especially feelings of profound guilt. This is why researchers have found that, even in combat when their own lives are at risk, a surprising number of soldiers still avoid killing by, for instance, intentionally firing their weapons too high.[87] To counter this, military organizations use psychological conditioning and combat training to "throw off the moral inhibitions" soldiers arrive with.[88] "Battleproofing" them means cultivating harshness, emotional distance, obedience, and seeing the enemy as inferior objects of disgust, hatred, and vengeance. Desensitization and euphemisms — "engaging targets" rather than killing persons — allow soldiers to "deny the humanity of the victim" of their violence. These methods all provide what Grossman describes as "prepackaged denial defense mechanisms" that allow a soldier to "deny to himself that he is actually killing another human being."[89] As the mother of one American participant in the My Lai massacre put it, "I sent them a good boy and they sent me back a murderer."[90]

Since warfare fosters violent dehumanization, it's not surprising that it can descend into what Bourke calls the "carnivalesque," a cruel celebration of brutality and bloodshed.[91] Genghis Khan infamously said, "Happiness lies in conquering your enemies, in driving them in front of you, in taking their property, in savouring their despair, in raping their wives and daughters."⁹² In World War I, some Allied veterans called bayonetting Germans "gorgeously satisfying" and "beautiful," while a mortar officer described "the happiest moment of my life" when his shot landed and he "saw bodies or parts of bodies go up in the air, and heard the desperate yelling of the wounded." American soldiers in Vietnam recalled, "I enjoyed the shooting and the killing. I was literally turned on when I saw a gook get shot," and, "It was encouraged to cut ears off, to cut the nose off, to cut the guy's penis off. A female, you cut her breasts off."⁹³ A helicopter gunner in the same war said: "I had enjoyed killing the three Vietcong who ran from the tree line near the village. Feeling like a glorious bird of prey swooping down, I watched the mini-gun rounds splash through the paddy toward the running men, then ripping and tearing their bodies to lifelessness."⁹⁴ During the Iraq War, General James Mattis, who would go on to be the US secretary of defense, simply said of war: "It's fun to shoot some people."⁹⁵ And normally a person getting a human skull in the mail would be horrified, but during World War II, a woman who received one of a dead Japanese soldier from her boyfriend fighting in the Pacific, signed by him with the words "a good Jap—a dead one," posed proudly with it for *Life* magazine.⁹⁶

All this confirms Simone Weil's observation, in her essay on the *Iliad*, that the "final secret of war" is its fundamental dehumanization. Its brutality transforms persons into things—mere objects, soulless bodies, animals to be slaughtered.⁹⁷ One veteran of World War I said "it was no place for a human being to be, really," and a marine in Vietnam dismissed atrocities against civilians, saying "it wasn't like they were humans." An infantry officer in World War II spoke of feeding soldiers into battle to be killed: "You use them up: they're material." Colonel David Hackworth, who fought in both Korea and Vietnam, described combat as "like working in a slaughterhouse. At first the blood, the gore, gets to you. But after a while you don't see it, you don't smell it, you don't feel it." A mother who lost her children in the massacre of civilians at Srebrenica during the Bosnian War said of herself and similar mothers: "We've been dead for a long time. Only our bodies are present."⁹⁸

Echoing Catholic teaching when it points to how such dehumanizing violence undermines the very things a just and humane society requires, observers and participants are frequently struck by how war corrodes kindness, compassion, tenderness, respect, joy, hope, and similar virtues.[99] Erasmus said that war "overwhelms, extinguishes, abolishes whatever is cheerful, whatever is happy and beautiful," and Hedges writes, "Stay long enough in war and real love, real tenderness and connection, becomes nearly impossible."[100] In World War I, one soldier recalled that "one had to be callous," while another wrote to his wife, saying: "I have no compunction, no sympathy. . . . I can't be bothered to waste tears." Commenting on the mass starvation of Leningrad's population in World War II, a German officer commented, "Sentimentality would be out of place." General Sherman said it was necessary to "make old and young, rich and poor, feel the hard hand of war," while General Patton told his soldiers that when they met the enemy "show him no mercy." Perhaps Heidi Baruch, a nurse in the Vietnam War, put it best: "When you live in an environment of hate and anger, you become hate and anger."[101]

— We can see, then, how those who experience war close-up confirm Catholic teaching's critique of its brutal dehumanization. While modern war does not necessarily kill a higher ratio of civilians to soldiers compared with wars of the past, Catholic teaching is correct to emphasize the frightening scale of death and destruction modern weapons can produce for both combatants and noncombatants alike. The Catholic case against war is especially clear-eyed in identifying mass killing as its central feature, in pointing to its devastating impact on those who survive it, and in cataloging its physical, social, economic, and environmental wreckage.

CHAPTER 2

WAR'S FALSE PROMISES AND THE POWER OF NONVIOLENCE

According to Catholic teaching, war has a remarkable power to distort thinking, to convince people that it is necessary, effective, and righteous, that war is the only realistic option and those who disagree are hopelessly utopian. But for the Vatican this gets things exactly backward. It is faith in war's power that is naïve and dangerous. True realism is recognizing that war does not deliver what it promises and instead makes things much worse.

While, as we saw in the introduction, Catholic teaching may still allow for armed force in certain extreme circumstances, it is now far more likely to question justifications for war and its effectiveness. Surveying wars around the world, John Paul II puts the case this way: "Violence is a lie, for it goes against the truth of our faith, the truth of our humanity. Violence destroys what it claims to defend: the dignity, the life, the freedom of human beings." In *Centesimus Annus*, he argues that history shows the folly of putting one's faith in armed force "in the name of political realism."[1] Francis echoes this, writing in *Fratelli Tutti*, "The truth is that violence has no basis in our fundamental religious convictions, but only in their distortion." He points to how often wars are rashly deemed both necessary and moral under false pretenses and the "manipulation of information," creating even greater evils than those they claim to solve. The true reality of war should be seen in its actual impact on victims rather than in the deceptive promises of its advocates.[2]

Reflecting on war, Francis writes, "We need to stop and ask ourselves what has led our world to see conflict as something normal." The answer for church teaching is that "the force of arms is deceptive," promising a "false sense of security" based on the "illusion" of safety through military might. This is "senseless and myopic" and "a kind of collective hysteria." War is driven by such things as ambition, hatred, resentful nationalism, a "thirst for power," and a "desire to dominate." But its primary source is fear, which distorts thinking and drives people to put their trust in armed force. According to John Paul II, "we must repudiate the logic" that leads to such thinking.[3]

Such a repudiation begins with rejecting war as an effective solution to conflict. John Paul II writes: "Recent history clearly shows the failure of recourse to violence as a means for resolving political and social problems. War destroys, it does not build up; it weakens the moral foundations of society and creates further divisions and long-lasting tensions. And yet the news continues to speak of wars and armed conflicts, and of their countless victims. How often have my Predecessors and I myself called for an end to these horrors!"[4] Elsewhere, he declares that the violence of war "never solves problems," that "war never helps the human community," that while war pursues "an apparent short-term gain, it involves a real and permanent loss," and, finally, that "nothing is resolved by war; on the contrary, everything is placed in jeopardy by war."[5]

Francis makes similar points when he condemns the world's "wars and conflicts that bring only death and destruction in their wake," when he declares that "violence is not the cure for our broken world," and when he denounces both war and the death penalty as "false answers that do not resolve the problems they are meant to solve and ultimately do no more than introduce new elements of destruction in the fabric of national and global society." For him, "War is never the way."⁶

This theme of war's not only being ineffective but actually making things worse appears regularly in Vatican documents.⁷ Francis declares that "every war leaves our world worse than it was before" and that "war does not devastate the present only, but the future of society as well." He and earlier popes emphasize in particular the "uncontrollable" forces that war unleashes. Paul VI argues that these "engender new injustices, introduce new inequities and bring new disasters" and that war "engenders new forms of oppression and enslavement which are often harder to bear than those from which they claimed to bring freedom." And John Paul II declares that war "leaves behind a trail of resentment and hatred, thus making it all the more difficult to find a just solution of the very problems which provoked the war."⁸

While traditional just war theory tends to focus on the short-term morality of particular wars, contemporary Catholic teaching is much more likely to examine the long-term effects of war itself, especially the way wars sow the seeds of future conflicts, creating cycles of violence that actually make communities less secure.⁹ The Second Vatican Council compares war to an "infection" that continues to spread unless stopped, and Paul VI writes, "The Church cannot accept violence, especially the force of arms . . . because she knows that violence always provokes violence." In opposing the US-led war against Iraq in 1991, John Paul II actually predicted its even bloodier sequel, warning that "a peace obtained by arms could only prepare new acts of violence." And in his 2000 message for the World Day of Peace, he states, "The twentieth century bequeaths to us above all else a warning: wars are often the cause of further wars because they fuel deep hatreds, create situations of injustice and trample upon people's dignity and rights." Francis too emphasizes "the spiral of vengeance" and "the vicious circle" of bloodshed created by war, arguing that "war begets war, violence begets violence." Since existing wars create "new and worse wars in the future," the world must "break this cycle."¹⁰

Its many statements on the arms trade are good illustrations of the Vatican's critique of war's fueling cycles of violence that worsen rather than prevent conflict and insecurity.[11] Catholic teaching regularly condemns what Benedict XVI calls "this baleful commerce" that makes war more likely by accelerating "instability, tension and conflict." The Second Vatican Council argues that building up arms is "not a safe way to preserve steady peace" and "is an utterly treacherous trap for humanity," and Paul VI states, "The arms race institutionalizes disorder." In *Evangelium Vitae*, John Paul II decries "the scandalous arms trade, which spawns the many armed conflicts which stain our world with blood," and in one of his World Day of Peace messages, he points out that the problem is not just heavy armaments or weapons of mass destruction: "Seeds of war are also being spread by the massive and uncontrolled proliferation of small arms and light weapons."[12]

— If war is deceptive and ineffective and only makes things worse by feeding cycles of violence, what are the alternatives? Catholic teaching's primary answers are the larger international and institutional methods detailed in the next two chapters—greater global governance, diplomacy and mediation, international organizations and norms, and addressing the underlying roots of war through economic and political development. But over the last several decades, the Vatican has also increasingly endorsed grassroots nonviolent resistance by average citizens as a direct alternative to armed force, considering it both more moral and more effective in protecting peace and security.

As far back as Vatican II, the council declared that "we cannot fail to praise those who renounce the use of violence in the vindication of their rights," and this emphasis has only grown with popes since.[13] John Paul II regularly highlights how nonviolence can effectively "counter the armed aggressor." In *Centesimus Annus*, he points to the failures of armed force in solving the conflict of the Cold War, writing: "Instead, it has been overcome by the non-violent commitment of people who, while always refusing to yield to the force of power, succeeded time after time in finding effective ways of bearing witness to the truth. This disarmed the adversary, since violence always needs to justify itself through deceit, and to appear, however falsely, to be defending a right or responding to a threat posed by others." And reflecting on the close of the twentieth century, he states:

> We cannot fail to remember the countless men and women who have contributed to the affirmation and the solemn proclamation of human rights, and who have helped to defeat the various forms of totalitarianism, to put an end to colonialism, to develop democracy and to establish the great international organizations. Those who built their lives on the value of non-violence have given us a luminous and prophetic example. Their example of integrity and loyalty, often to the point of martyrdom, has provided us with rich and splendid lessons.

Concluding that "in the world there is too much violence, too much injustice, and therefore that this situation cannot be overcome except by countering it with more love, with more goodness," Benedict XVI praises active nonviolence as a way to overcome evil by "breaking the chain of injustice." And in his landmark 2017 World Day of Peace Message entitled *Nonviolence: A Style of Politics for Peace*, Francis declares that "active nonviolence" does not "mean surrender, lack of involvement and passivity," but it is instead "more powerful than violence." For Francis, "while the force of arms is deceptive," the "decisive and consistent practice of nonviolence has produced impressive results," and he points to the role of women in particular as leaders of such efforts.[14]

WAR'S FIRST CASUALTY IS TRUTH

A central theme of *War Is a Force That Gives Us Meaning*, Chris Hedges's account of his experiences reporting from combat zones around the world, is how they are awash in falsehoods. War creates a "warped version of reality," one that "distorts memory, corrupts language, and infects everything around it." He details how propaganda and outlandish conspiracy theories about enemy groups flourish, how history books, school curricula, and public exhibits get quickly rewritten to prop up new "national myths" that feed a kind of "collective amnesia." Fear, hatred, and dividing people into allies and enemies, "a black and white tableau of them and us," means war "suspends thought, especially self-critical thought." For Hedges, the cynical "destruction of honest inquiry, the notion that one fact is as good as the next, is one of the most disturbing consequences of war." Of course, these dynamics can exist outside of war zones, but they become enormously magnified within them, since "war entails lying, often on a massive scale."[15]

Lies and coverups are a regular feature of war—from inflated body counts, to rosy reports of battlefield success, to suppressing or coopting the press, to hiding atrocities committed by one's side, even while exaggerating those committed by the other.[16] The My Lai massacre of 500 Vietnamese civilians, most women and children, which also included mass rape, was reported by the US military as a routine engagement where 128 enemy soldiers were killed. During World War I, Turkish officials referred to mass deportations of Armenians, a prelude to their genocide, as "restoration of order in the war zone by military measures," and a century later the country still denies the genocide ever took place. And not only does Pakistan's official military history make no mention of the mass killing and rape its soldiers carried out against civilians during the Bangladesh independence war, but the country's school curriculum actually implies Pakistan won the war (when in fact its forces were defeated and it lost roughly half its territory).[17]

As these examples illustrate, and consistent with what we saw in the last chapter, there is a powerful tendency in war to hide the reality of its lethal violence. Whether by denial, erasure, or obscuring through euphemisms such as "neutralizing targets" or "collateral damage," the killing at war's core is often buried under what Dave Grossman, the military psychologist, calls "a cultural conspiracy of forgetfulness, distortion, and lies."[18] In his study of war and public opinion, John Tirman concludes that war depends on a particular "epistemology" that deflects attention away from its killing to cultivate a powerful "capacity to forget the carnage."[19] It's not that popular images of war completely ignore its violence, but rather that they emphasize excitement, courage, and honor, while downplaying its meaningless slaughter, industrial-scale killing, and massive suffering by innocents. For instance, even video games that pride themselves on their "realism" systematically erase the reality of civilian deaths in war.[20]

This gap between image and reality is a hallmark of modern writing about war, as soldiers lured by the promise of adventure, heroism, and serving a noble cause become disenchanted by what they actually experience.[21] Reflecting on the contrast between what he was told about war before joining the US military and what he really encountered in Vietnam, Manuel Carvalho said: "They don't tell you that side. . . . They don't tell you the reality. . . . I was being conned."[22] And after urging young men to find glory fighting in World War I, only to see his own son killed alongside much of his generation, Rudyard Kipling famously wrote that when soldiers died it was because their fathers lied.[23]

— Catholic teaching is correct, then, when it identifies lying as central to the conduct and experience of warfare. It is also correct to connect falsehood to the onset of wars in the first place. Erasmus noted that leaders regularly seek "the varnish with which they endeavor to disguise their mischievous iniquity."[24] Blending appeals to noble sentiments such as security, peace, or liberty with a strong dose of nationalist pride makes for a powerful varnish. The Nazi leader Hermann Goering famously observed how easy it is to build public support for war: "All you have to do is tell them they are being attacked and denounce the pacifists for lack of patriotism." And a North Korean colonel states of his military today: "We want to achieve world peace."[25] It's not that every single side in every single armed conflict relies on bogus claims—sometimes security or freedom really is at stake. It's just that genuinely noble causes tend to be the exception. Even in defending the possibility of a war for the right reasons, the philosopher Elizabeth Anscombe acknowledges that "wars have mostly been mere wickedness on both sides."[26]

In *The New American Militarism*, Andrew Bacevich uses the contemporary United States to illustrate how falsehoods so often pave the way for wars. Defining militarism as "a romanticized view of soldiers, a tendency to see military power as the truest measure of national greatness, and outsized expectations regarding the efficacy of force," he explores how it has "beguiled Americans" into supporting disastrous wars such as the 2003 invasion of Iraq. Central to this militarism is the "myth" that the US military fights to protect Americans from attack and to uphold national values such as peace and freedom, when in fact its real job is self-interested "imperial policing" around the world. Militarism supplies the fiction that American soldiers are "bringing peace and light to troubled corners of the earth rather than pushing ever outward the perimeter of an American empire."[27]

Bacevich's myth, which he sees rooted in a false "sentimentalized version of the American military experience," shapes the ways both the American public and soldiers themselves view overseas wars such as the one in Iraq. One soldier after surviving a battle with local militias in Iraq that almost killed him said, "If I had to die it would be defending my country," and another received a photo from a youth football team in Colorado, one that had decided to dedicate their season to him, in which all the kids yelled "freedom" as it was snapped. Others who had suffered terrible injuries fighting in Iraq were told by the chairman of the Joint Chiefs of Staff that they had given their limbs so that Americans could be free.[28]

The way militarism undermines truth goes beyond outright falsehoods. Even more insidious is how it misleads by distorting thinking. For Bacevich, building and idealizing a large and expensive military causes leaders to overuse it, usually in misguided ways. It becomes an "all-purpose tool" suitable for any problem or crisis, even if it is, in truth, poorly suited for the job. It causes policymakers to attach unreasonable expectations to military force, dismissing unintended consequences that can actually render a country less safe.[29] Once war becomes the default option, leaders continue to rely on it and funnel it more resources, even if it doesn't deliver as promised, proves less effective than alternatives, and diverts attention from other genuine needs.[30] In the 1970s, the prime minister of Pakistan was so intent on developing nuclear weapons to match India's, no matter the financial cost to his people, that he said they would "eat grass" if necessary.[31] Under militarism's misleading logic, even its failures can cause leaders to double down. Historians have demonstrated, for instance, that in World War I militarism not only contributed to starting the conflict by making Europe's leaders overly optimistic about their respective military prowess but also, once the war did not go to plan and turned into a bloody stalemate, led to a classic sunk-cost fallacy, where the growing loss of life and treasure demanded pouring in even more of both, so that the previous losses would not be in vain. As James Sheehan writes, "This was the vicious circle in which all the belligerents were trapped: the more sacrifices they demanded, the more essential victory became, which in turn required more sacrifices."[32]

Sometimes militarism's distorted reasoning becomes so extreme that it slips into a kind of magical thinking. Bacevich argues that even as war regularly proves itself "ungovernable" once unleashed, militarism seduces people into thinking they can "make war do their bidding." It can become "utopian" or "eschatological" in its far-fetched promises to remake the world.[33] Indeed, observers have identified a long tradition, from superpowers to terrorist groups, of thinking that an intense jolt of righteous violence will somehow cleanse the world of evil and usher in a new and better order.[34] As John Howard Yoder once remarked, "There is no more utopian institution than an idealistic war."[35]

WAR'S POOR PERFORMANCE RECORD

Militarism's distortions create a powerful tendency to overestimate war's effectiveness. A central theme in comparative work on the onset of armed conflict is miscalculation. Again and again, leaders misjudge their own military power, expecting a quick and decisive victory, only to become mired in disastrous wars that end in failure.[36] From the Athenian expedition against Sicily in 415 BCE to the outbreak of World War I over twenty-three centuries later, overconfidence routinely leads war planners into catastrophes. More recent examples include leaders in Saudi Arabia and Russia launching military operations, in Yemen and Ukraine respectively, that they expected to be over in a matter of weeks, only to become bogged down in much longer, bloodier, and inclusive conflicts. And, of course, Americans have their own post-9/11 wars, where expectations of quick victories and being welcomed as liberators gave way to calamitous realities. When the longest war in US history finally ended with the American withdrawal from Afghanistan in 2021 and the Taliban back in power, Steve Coll and Adam Entous summed up two decades of violent failure as "a dispiriting record of misjudgment, hubris, and delusion from the very start."[37]

In *Why We Fight*, his analysis of how wars begin, Christopher Blattman identifies misperception problems as a key factor. He uses the concept of "naïve realism" to describe leaders who assume they see situations objectively but in fact fail to adequately understand their opponents. This leads to overconfidence in the efficacy of force to deter or defeat those opponents, when in reality it usually leads to escalating cycles of violence. Such misperceptions become even more dramatic when a country's leaders all share an ethnic, nationalist, religious, or other group identity, have a deep suspicion of their opponents, and lack voices offering nonviolent alternatives. All this increases the risk of reckless action that leads to military failures that should have been foreseen but were not.[38]

— This is not to say that all wars are unsuccessful. Catholic teaching may be right that war itself is always a loss for humanity, but in a narrower sense warfare can achieve its objectives, at least in the short term. Sometimes those who fight wars do get what they want out of them—new territory or resources, national liberation, control of the government. But this actually happens less frequently than many assume. War and military power enjoy reputations for effectiveness that they do not deserve.

Blattman concludes that most wars are lose-lose affairs: "War's destructiveness means that both sides are almost always better off finding a peaceful split than going to war."[39] Many wars end with no side achieving its objectives, and even when one side does, its opponents obviously do not, all of which adds up to a pretty poor overall success rate. And having a large and powerful military actually doesn't help. It leads to a country's getting into more rather than fewer armed conflicts, and it does not increase the odds of success in those conflicts. Sheer military power has *no predictive impact* on whether or not a country wins a war. So-called great powers have long records of failing to defeat seemingly weaker opponents, and military operations beyond their borders tend to produce blowback, when the death and destruction brought to foreign populations only creates more grievances, hostility, and deadly retaliation, sowing the seeds of future wars. The US military, for instance, has the power to bomb almost any location on earth at will, and it has, over the last several decades, used this power widely and frequently to try and shape behavior by other countries and nonstate groups alike. Yet not only has this regular bombing almost always failed to change such behavior; it has generated the kinds of violent resentment and reprisal that actually make Americans less safe and produce new rounds of conflict. One study of US military strikes concluded that fewer than 6 percent achieved their political objectives. As armed conflict researchers David Cortright, Conor Seyle, and Kristen Wall write, "When judged by the ability to achieve political goals, most uses of military force are ineffective."[40]

While many assume a powerful military provides greater protection for a country's population, the reality is much different. Worldwide, militaries are more likely to actually threaten public security, carrying out internal coups and enforcing oppressive domestic dictatorships far more often than actually defending the country against external threats.[41] Take Latin America, where armed forces rarely if ever fight against those of other countries. Historically, they are far more likely to act as agents of domestic oppression while draining public resources and abetting political corruption. An exception is Costa Rica, which in 1949 abolished its military, diverting its spending into education and healthcare. Today it is more prosperous, secure, and free compared to its neighbors, and it regularly tops world rankings of the happiest nations.[42]

The arms trade, which we have seen comes in for sharp criticism from the Vatican, offers another example of how more military power does not equal more peace and security. Historically, arms buildups, and higher levels of defense spending generally, significantly increase the chances of war between countries, especially if other risk factors are present. However, this relationship declined significantly following World War II, which some researchers attribute to the dynamics of the Cold War and the unique threats posed by nuclear weapons.[43] The impact on civil wars, which are far more common today, is more consistent across time. Higher military spending and arms transfers into areas already at risk of intrastate conflict make the outbreak of wars significantly more likely. They also cause such wars to last longer and kill more people. Rather than a deterrent, building up military capacity acts instead as an accelerant to civil wars.[44] Researchers in this area generally agree that while arms buildups and transfers are not an independent cause of armed conflict, as Catholic teaching sometimes suggests, they do make it more likely and more deadly when other risk factors are also present, which is usually the case when such buildups and transfers occur.

— Let's take a closer look at war's track record in some areas where it most often seems necessary: defeating foreign aggression or domestic dictatorships, safeguarding peaceful democracies, and preventing mass atrocities such as genocide. This is important not only for assessing war's overall effectiveness but in comparing it to nonviolent civil resistance efforts across these same areas in our next section.

Start with people taking up arms to liberate themselves from foreign occupiers or overthrow domestic dictators. How well does war work here? Not particularly well, it turns out. Large empirical studies of hundreds of cases stretching back over a century show that in these situations war succeeds only around 25 percent of the time in aggregate, and this success rate has been steadily dropping over the last fifty years, falling all the way down to below 10 percent in the last few decades.[45] Armed force does sometimes stop foreign aggressors or topple tyrannical regimes, but not in the vast majority of cases. Failure is far more likely.

And what happens in those relatively few cases where such armed force does succeed? The result is almost always a new dictatorship and an elevated risk of renewed warfare. The data show that only a tiny minority, around 5 percent, of successful wars against foreign occupation or domestic tyranny actually result in democratic regimes, and most relapse into a cycle of violence that puts them back in a civil war again within a few years.[46] So while such successful wars are already rare, those that both succeed and produce peaceful democracies are almost nonexistent.[47]

How well does war protect vulnerable people from the most severe abuses such as ethnic cleansing or genocide? Researchers who study such mass atrocities have found that warfare itself significantly raises the odds that they will occur. As Erica Chenoweth writes, "Mass killings, including genocide, are most common during wars."[48] Such atrocities almost always occur during an armed conflict that is already underway and unfold as part of its cycle of increasing violence. Regimes facing armed insurgencies become more likely to engage in mass killing, doing so in around 70 percent of cases. Here is Chenoweth again: "Armed struggle is the most robust predictor of government-led mass killings." So such insurgencies, in addition to having low odds of success, actually increase the chances that atrocities, including escalation to genocide, will occur.[49]

One response to mass atrocities already underway or seemingly about to occur is armed intervention by outside parties. Advocates of a "responsibility to protect" argue that members of the international community should, under certain conditions, use military force to defend vulnerable populations against ethnic cleansing, genocide, or other forms of mass violence (as we have seen, Vatican statements have in the past sometimes offered qualified endorsements of such action too). The United Nations formally endorsed this principle in 2005.[50]

Some critics dismiss armed humanitarian interventions as mere cover for powerful countries to engage in self-interested aggression, but even good-faith efforts face daunting problems, ones countries tend to underestimate, and they have achieved few clear-cut successes.[51] These interventions almost always mean taking sides in an ongoing civil war, which poses a problem since outside powers that do so, for whatever reason, rarely achieve their objectives, instead only prolonging conflicts, further piling up their tolls of death and destruction, and almost never producing stable democracies. Intervening on one side also undercuts the nonaligned position that, as we will see in the next chapter, is important in helping to end armed conflicts.[52] Furthermore, most mass atrocities happen before outside military powers can realistically intervene, and once those interventions are underway, the death and destruction that inevitably comes with warfare can undercut the interventions' humanitarian legitimacy.[53] Finally, there is an underlying moral hazard problem: the practice can actually encourage groups to launch armed rebellions against regimes in the hopes of then attracting an outside intervention. So military interventions can establish a pattern that actually sparks new wars, particularly the type where the very kind of mass killing they are intended to prevent is most likely to occur.[54]

Measuring the success of armed interventions to prevent or stop mass atrocities can be difficult. Aside from the problem of getting reliable information on the actual levels of risk before interventions and the number of lives saved by them, we don't know what would have happened had such interventions not taken place, especially since they foreclose the kind of nonmilitary alternatives that we will consider below.[55] In his analysis of several case studies of armed humanitarian interventions, Taylor Seybolt concludes that some can be deemed successful, such as the 1999 Australian-led effort in East Timor, but mixed results or outright failure is more common. While the interventions he studied were most successful in saving lives by delivering humanitarian aid to conflict zones, they were, paradoxically, least successful in directly protecting victims from mass violence.[56]

The 2011 NATO-led military intervention in Libya, the first explicitly authorized by the United Nations Security Council under the responsibility-to-protect doctrine, is a good illustration of the pitfalls such interventions face. It was launched against the Qaddafi government, during a civil war, to stop its purportedly imminent mass slaughter of civilians in the city of Benghazi, though the British government, which participated in the intervention, later concluded that the direct threat to civilians was exaggerated by those hoping to attract military assistance to the rebel side against the regime.[57] The intervention did tip the military balance toward the rebels, leading to the regime's fall and Qaddafi's execution, but its aftermath was disastrous, ushering in far more bloodshed than the intervention was designed to prevent. It turned a relatively stable country, albeit one ruled by a dictator, into a failed state plagued by chronic, multisided warfare. The subsequent conflict was marked by widespread civilian death and massive refugee flows. Furthermore, again confirming Catholic teaching's association of war with ongoing cycles of violence, the warfare in Libya expanded across the region as fighters and their weapons spread to neighboring countries, bringing new wars and instability to them in turn. Indeed, jihadist militias across north and central Africa, such as Boko Haram, were among the intervention's primary beneficiaries.[58]

Catholic teaching is correct, then, when it emphasizes war's overall ineffectiveness. Wars that achieve the goals of those who fight them are the exception. Most warfare fails most of the time. Fortunately, Catholic teaching is also correct that there are alternatives with a better record of success. The most immediate of these is nonviolent civil resistance, and a wealth of recent research allows us to see direct comparisons between its efficacy and that of armed force.

NONVIOLENT CIVIL RESISTANCE AS A MORE EFFECTIVE ALTERNATIVE

The emergence of coordinated unarmed resistance movements is one of the most important global developments of the last century. The techniques these movements rely upon have deep historical roots, but it was twentieth-century leaders such as India's Mohandas Gandhi, the Philippines' Corazon Aquino, and Poland's Lech Walesa that drew them together to form a new and potent political tool.

Nonviolent civil resistance is based on a simple insight about the nature of power: leaders need people to do as they are told. From substitute teachers to store managers to generals to monarchs, authority depends on cooperation. Normally, leaders can count on this, because people believe in their legitimacy, or accept it out of habit, or just want to avoid being punished for disobedience. But sometimes, if enough people simultaneously stop obeying, a leader's power can evaporate. This is what the influential theorist of nonviolent action Gene Sharp calls "the Achilles heel of all governments."[59]

Even the most cruel, dictatorial regimes can't function without a vast array of people—bureaucrats, police, soldiers, bankers, transportation and energy workers, shopkeepers, teachers, religious leaders, food producers, and other ordinary citizens of all kinds—doing their jobs and contributing to the system's continuing operation. Nonviolent civil resistance happens when a critical mass of these people stop doing so, and instead shift their usual cooperation to active noncooperation and disruption. This can take the form of strikes, boycotts, stay-at-homes, mass demonstrations, blockades, refusing to pay taxes or rents, setting up parallel governments, and other methods. It can bring entire societies to a halt. And if a regime resorts to violence against nonviolent protestors, it often backfires, spreading and intensifying the noncooperation. When this results in security force defection—when ordinary police officers and soldiers ignore or refuse orders to use violence against the population—a regime's final way to secure cooperation disappears and its power collapses.[60]

In addition to the cases of India, the Philippines, and Poland above, such unarmed resistance movements have proven successful in places such as Serbia, Chile, South Africa, Georgia, Nepal, Algeria, Sudan, Thailand, and Lithuania. They have also failed, however, in places such as China, Iran, Russia, Bahrain, Belarus, Turkey, and Syria. And such movements are increasing in frequency. There have been more instances in the first two decades of the twenty-first century than in all of the twentieth century combined, and they are now the norm for resistance movements, far outnumbering instances of armed force.[61] Given its growing ubiquity and that it succeeds in some cases but fails in others, the fact that we now have a growing body of sophisticated empirical research on nonviolent civil resistance, including how it compares to warfare, is extremely valuable.

— Let's start again with people trying to liberate themselves from foreign occupiers or overthrow domestic dictators. In their landmark 2011 book, *Why Civil Resistance Works*, which did more than any other to launch the current surge in comparative empirical work on nonviolent resistance, Chenoweth and Maria Stephan examine over three hundred cases of violent and nonviolent movements and conclude that on average nonviolent ones are twice as effective. (More recently, in 2021's *Civil Resistance*, Chenoweth confirms this gap using an updated and expanded set of over six hundred cases stretching back over a century.) As we saw in the last section, armed resistance to foreign occupation or domestic tyranny succeeds on average only around 25 percent of the time, but nonviolent civil resistance succeeds in just over 50 percent of cases.[62] With the recent explosion of nonviolent movements—many rushed and poorly planned—and target regimes' learning to adjust to them, their success rate has dropped to around 34 percent over the last decade or so. But with violent successes dropping even more, to below 10 percent, nonviolence is now actually three times as likely to succeed.[63] Other researchers confirm the greater efficacy of nonviolence in toppling dictators and preventing new ones from seizing power through coups.[64] Overthrowing occupiers and autocrats is difficult, which is why there is no guaranteed way to do so, but if you want to try it, nonviolent civil resistance gives you two to three times better odds of success. In the words of Chenoweth and Stephan, "Among campaigns seeking regime change or liberation from foreign occupation, nonviolent resistance has been strategically superior."[65]

Nonviolence's superiority holds regardless of a target regime's character (democratic, authoritarian, mixed) and how it reacts. Crucially, whether or not regimes respond with violence, and how intense that violence is, actually makes no difference to the superior success rate of unarmed resistance. Nonviolent movements still overcome violent responses better than armed ones. And those carrying out nonviolent resistance can increase their odds even more by planning for violent responses ahead of time, by alternating tactics between those relying on concentration (such as sit-ins and demonstrations) and those relying on dispersion (such as boycotts and general strikes), and by preparing for leadership succession at all levels in case of imprisonment or death. A good example of such flexible tactics is the work of South Africa's United Democratic Front in the struggle against apartheid.[66]

One of the best predictors of whether a resistance movement, violent or nonviolent, will succeed is how much participation it draws from the local population. This is where nonviolent campaigns have an enormous advantage; they average four times as many participants as violent ones.[67] This should not be surprising. With a wider array of methods and lower participation barriers, they are more likely to draw on a wider and more socially diverse base of support—older as well as younger, women as well as men, the disabled, parents of young children, and others less likely to take up arms. The ability to involve women is especially significant in boosting their success rates, as is evident, for instance, in movements from Chile to the Philippines to Sudan. And if a movement is able to attract just 3.5 percent of a population as active participants, it almost never fails.[68]

More widespread, socially diverse participation allows unarmed civil resistance to better create what Srdja Popovic, a leader of the successful nonviolent movement that toppled the genocidal dictator Slobodan Milošević in Serbia, calls the "line of division" in a population, maximizing people and groups on the opposition side while increasingly isolating the regime and its supporters. This dynamic, which Stephan says is able to "extend the nonviolent battlefield," is more likely to break off people in key areas that the regime needs to survive, its "pillars of support" such as the army, religious leaders, civil servants, media figures, professional associations, or economic elites that give it access to financial markets. Armed movements, on the other hand, tend to rally regime supporters around it. This is also why nonviolent civil resistance is better able to spark security force defection; soldiers and police officers are more likely to refuse to shoot if they are not being attacked themselves, and if their own friends, neighbors, religious leaders, and family members are urging them not to. A Serbian police officer explained his refusal to fire at protestors when ordered to by Milošević's regime, saying, "I knew my kids would be in the crowd."[69]

It is important to realize that the way nonviolent movements secure loyalty-shifts among people crucial to a regime's operation is not only through moral appeals but through self-interest as well. They increase the social and financial costs of continuing to support the government. And as a regime weakens, movements can create a tipping point; when people fear being caught on the wrong side when it goes down, they rush to abandon it, accelerating the collapse even more. Self-interest also shapes the response of the regime's leaders themselves. Since losing power to a nonviolent movement carries a much lower risk of being lined up and shot, leaders are more likely to negotiate an exit from power than when facing violent insurgencies.[70]

— What about the aftermath of nonviolent and violent campaigns against foreign occupation or domestic dictators that do succeed? In addition to unarmed instances being much quicker — averaging just over a year compared to five years for armed ones — they are much more likely to produce stable democratic regimes and avoid relapse into civil war. As Chenoweth and Stephan write, "Our statistical evidence suggests that countries in which violent insurgencies exist are more likely to backslide into authoritarianism or civil war than countries where nonviolent campaigns exist, which often become more stable, democratic regimes."[71]

The probability of a country being a democracy five years after a successful nonviolent campaign is almost 60 percent compared to only around 5 percent for successful violent ones, a more than tenfold difference. Indeed, it is extraordinarily rare in the modern world for a country to transition from an autocratic to democratic form of government without the kind of mass unarmed protest that accompanies nonviolent resistance campaigns.[72] Not only is nonviolent civil resistance far more likely to produce democracies, but these democracies are more durable and score higher on measures of "democratic quality," which look at such things as broad political participation and protection of basic human rights. There is a similar dynamic with coups; those defeated by nonviolent resistance methods are more likely to result in stable democracies. As the researcher Jonathan Pinckney concludes, "Relative to other means of achieving political change, nonviolent actions are the most effective way of ensuring that a country will move from a non-democratic political system to one that is democratic and protects political freedoms."[73] And because countries emerging from successful unarmed resistance campaigns are less likely to experience renewed conflict and civil war, they enjoy greater economic growth and a higher average life expectancy than countries emerging from successful armed campaigns.[74]

Remarkably, even countries where unarmed resistance campaigns *fail* are less likely to experience future civil wars and are four times as likely to transition to democracy within five years as those with successful violent campaigns.[75] Yes, that's right, even unsuccessful nonviolent civil resistance is significantly more likely to set a country on the road to peaceful democracy than successful violent force!

— Let's turn to what we know about nonviolent action and mass atrocities, including genocide. In most cases, regimes use violent repression against both armed and unarmed resistance campaigns. This includes beatings, arbitrary detention, torture, assassination, and disappearances. However, the most extreme forms of violence, mass killings of civilians, including killings that escalate to genocide, are more common when regimes confront armed campaigns. As Chenoweth writes, "Armed movements operating in wartime contexts are more likely to face genocidal violence than those that are unarmed." Widespread massacres of civilians suspected of supporting the opposition happen around three times as often in response to violent campaigns (68 percent of cases) as they do in response to nonviolent ones (23 percent of cases). Mass killing by the target regime, then, is the norm during armed campaigns but the exception during unarmed ones. And, of course, the resistance movement itself does not carry out massacres during nonviolent campaigns, but this does happen regularly during armed ones. Furthermore, because nonviolent resistance is also far less likely to generate new autocrats and civil wars, both of which are risk factors for mass atrocities, it also reduces the odds that such atrocities will happen in the future. Chenoweth sums up the results of all these factors: "Compared to armed resistance, nonviolent resistance significantly reduces the chance of mass killings."[76]

So nonviolent civil resistance itself, as opposed to taking up arms and fighting wars, is one way to help reduce the risk of genocide and other mass atrocities in the first place. Another is using the broader tools available to the international community that we will consider in the next two chapters, ones that also help prevent mass atrocities, including genocides, by shaping state and nonstate behavior and averting the kinds of conflicts where they are most likely to occur.

But what if such preventive steps still fail and mass atrocities have begun or seem imminent? We have seen that external armed interventions are not especially effective in such cases. Can nonviolent methods offer any direct alternatives? Since earlier action to prevent mass killings or the conflicts that spawn them in the first place is always better than trying to respond once they arrive, there are no methods guaranteed to always succeed; nonviolence faces many of the same limitations as violence when such a point has already been reached. Nonetheless, researchers have uncovered some promising findings that show the potential for nonviolent action to protect vulnerable people from mass atrocities, even in the most dangerous and violent circumstances.

Given the limits of armed interventions under the responsibility-to-protect principle, some scholars have suggested an alternative "obligation to assist" that mobilizes international support for local populations using nonviolent methods in conflict zones, especially since armed interventions tend to sideline such efforts.[77] This can include indirect support with publicity, logistics, and financial assistance, or even direct accompaniment through what is commonly called "unarmed civilian protection." This is where teams of trained international observers live among local populations at risk of mass killing. There is a growing body of evidence that these teams have a deterring and mediating impact, effectively reducing killing, displacement, and human rights abuses in situations where armed interventions fail. Stephan writes that such groups have successfully "saved lives, changed the behavior of armed groups, and made local peace and human rights work more possible." Such teams are currently deployed in dozens of conflict zones.[78]

These efforts succeed by amplifying rather than supplanting unarmed resistance by local people themselves. This is important, because such local resistance is more sustained and effective than large-scale interventions by outsiders.[79] Books such as *Opting Out of War*, by Mary Anderson and Marshall Wallace, and *Resisting War*, by Oliver Kaplan, draw on cases from dozens of countries around the world to detail how communities in war zones regularly rely on nonviolent methods to protect themselves from being branded enemies and targeted by regimes or armed insurgency groups.[80] These are not remote or strategically unimportant communities. They are similar to others that are dragged into conflicts and targeted for mass killing by one side or the other, except that these communities develop a variety of methods to defend themselves. Such methods include relying on respected community leaders, practicing inclusive decision-making, and planning ahead as a conflict looms. These communities cultivate a group identity separate from those dividing participants in the armed conflict around them. They emphasize internal unity, mutual aid, and maintaining high morale, even in the face of suffering. They do not respond to provocations from outside groups, even violent ones. They make their unity and neutrality in the conflict clear and consistent from the start, often signaled in public marches and demonstrations, but also conveyed directly through regular communication and negotiation with armed parties. These communities group together in large numbers when danger looms, maintain nonviolent discipline, and demonstrate their willingness to cause disruption through noncooperation if threatened. They find ways to communicate to participants in the armed conflict that it is far less costly and troublesome to just leave them alone. These methods cannot absolutely guarantee a community won't experience mass atrocities during an armed conflict, but they significantly reduce the risk of its happening. Anderson and Wallace write that "such capacities exist—even in warring areas—far more often than is usually recognized or acknowledged."[81]

Even when mass atrocities do occur, and violence seems to dominate, we can still see ordinary acts of nonviolence mitigating its impact. All genocides include stories of ordinary people rescuing victims—hiding them, treating their wounds, smuggling them to safety. And while Christina Lamb's investigation of mass rape during warfare includes accounts of terrible violence, some of which we saw in the last chapter, it also details powerful stories of rescue, refuge, and medical and psychological care, usually by other women.[82]

Furthermore, building social awareness of and the capacity for nonviolent civil resistance has the potential to do even more. Mass atrocities depend on widespread collaboration. They are ongoing projects that need people to plan, coordinate, and operate them. Genocides in particular require large-scale cooperation to identify, capture, detain, and kill victims. They need local officials, police, civil servants, neighbors, and co-workers to participate. In cases where such people refuse to cooperate, genocidal violence fails, even if armed troops are attempting to carry it out—something true even in the midst of World War II in places such as Bulgaria, Denmark, parts of France, and elsewhere.[83]

— So, considering the data on nonviolent civil resistance in its entirety, it is clear that while it does not guarantee success, it is nonetheless consistently and significantly more effective than armed force. Catholic teaching is right to emphasize its potential as a direct alternative to warfare. And such alternatives are important. While armed force can sometimes achieve its objectives, its actual success rate is terrible, especially when it comes to securing lasting peace, security, and human rights. The Vatican is correct, then, in its overall focus on how wars and preparations for wars distort thinking, promise results they rarely deliver, and usually make things much worse.

CHAPTER 3

PREVENTING WAR THROUGH GREATER GLOBAL GOVERNANCE

Given war's death and suffering, its deceptions and cycles of violence, and its ineffectiveness compared to nonviolence, how can the world more effectively prevent war, reducing its frequency and terrible costs?

Catholic teaching's case against war includes a comprehensive strategy for doing so, one that emphasizes two broad areas. The first is closer international cooperation to address common problems, build mutual trust and shared norms, and strengthen alternatives to armed force for resolving conflicts. The second is removing the underlying roots of war by working for greater economic and political justice. We will examine the first area in this chapter, then turn to the second in the next chapter.

— According to the Vatican, the international community must use the globe's growing connectedness to foster more cooperation across borders, replacing conflict with collaboration. Church statements regularly invoke the "growing interdependence" of humanity created by globalization and the worldwide scope of contemporary challenges from development to the environment to public health.[1] As Benedict XVI stresses, globalization can "create new divisions within the human family" and intensify global problems such as inequality or climate change, but if "suitably understood and directed," globalization also offers humanity a "great opportunity" for unity and mutual assistance. If we are to do this, in the words of John Paul II, "interdependence must be transformed into solidarity."[2] Catholic teaching frequently stresses the growing awareness that the "good of the whole human family" is linked—that, as Francis puts it, "we are all in the same boat." John Paul II applauds "the fact that men and women in various parts of the world feel personally affected by the injustices and violations of human rights committed in distant countries, countries which perhaps they will never visit." This awareness indicates, as John XXIII states, that there is a "universal common good; the good, that is, of the whole human family."[3]

This universal common good is the basis of the church's call for the world's countries to recognize the many areas where their intertwined interests point toward shared goals. Dialogue around these helps build "mutual trust," encouraging engagement rather than competition and fear. Francis writes, "I repeat forcefully: it is neither a culture of confrontation nor a culture of conflict which builds harmony within and between peoples, but rather a culture of encounter and a culture of dialogue; this is the only way to peace."[4] Building trust through such encounters provides the foundation for sustained cooperation and mutual aid to address shared global challenges in ways that contribute to the common good of all.[5] John Paul II sums it up well: "In this way, the solidarity which we propose is the path to peace and at the same time to development. For world peace is inconceivable unless the world's leaders come to recognize that interdependence in itself demands the abandonment of the politics of blocs, the sacrifice of all forms of economic, military or political imperialism, and the transformation of mutual distrust into collaboration. This is precisely the act proper to solidarity among individuals and nations."[6]

How can this general call for greater global collaboration be translated into tangible action? Catholic teaching responds by emphasizing a range of methods embedded in stronger international governance. More effective cooperation for the global common good cannot happen without mechanisms to "promote, coordinate and direct it."[7] In *Pacem in Terris*, John XXIII writes: "Today the universal common good presents us with problems which are world-wide in their dimensions; problems, therefore, which cannot be solved except by a public authority with power, organization and means co-extensive with these problems, and with a world-wide sphere of activity."[8]

Vatican statements frequently use phrases such as "world authority," a "political authority exercised at the level of the international community," or "a new constitutional organization of the human family."[9] John Paul II explicitly sees this as "the next phase of the evolution of world politics." Just as countries gradually developed forms of political authority larger than local institutions to settle disputes and address common problems, the international community must continue to do the same.[10] This goal is described most fully by Benedict XVI in *Caritas in Veritate*, where he calls for "a political, juridical and economic order which can increase and give direction to international cooperation for the development of all peoples in solidarity." This requires "a true world political authority" with "real teeth." It must have the "authority to ensure compliance with its decisions" and be "vested with the effective power to ensure security for all, regard for justice, and respect for rights."[11]

The greater global governance the Vatican endorses requires that individual countries yield some of their sovereign power to international institutions, but it in no way sees them being replaced by some kind of single world government. John Paul II writes: "But let there be no misunderstanding. This does not mean writing the constitution of a global super-State." The principle of subsidiarity means that some matters should be addressed at the local or national levels, some at the international level, and some at multiple levels. Some issues are best handled by government bodies, others within civil society by nonstate actors, and others in combination. So, rather than supplanting governments or social institutions within individual countries, global political authority is embedded in a network of overlapping intergovernmental and nongovernmental organizations that work alongside those governments and institutions at the international level. This is a process already underway, one that can weave what Francis calls "an architecture of peace" into the world's growing web of intersecting international institutions.[12]

For Catholic teaching, this web contains a rich array of tools for international collaboration and dispute resolution. As far back as *Mater et Magistra* in 1961, popes have been praising "an ever-extending network of societies and organizations which set their sights beyond the aims and interests of individual countries and concentrate on the economic, social, cultural and political welfare of all nations throughout the world."[13] This includes the growing network of international nongovernmental organizations and transnational grassroots movements that make up global civil society. It also includes intergovernmental organizations that bring official representatives from multiple countries together in the many regional or worldwide bodies created by formal agreements, ones that usually incorporate monitoring and enforcement mechanisms as well. One of the most frequent themes in Catholic teaching is its celebration of the concrete work such groups do in bringing attention to and taking action on international issues—environmental protection, human rights, development, trade, security, conflict resolution, global health, human trafficking, famine, refugee assistance—and its calls to further support and strengthen such efforts.[14] It frequently warns, however, that these efforts must be truly inclusive, working for the global common good rather than being a vehicle for more powerful groups or countries to pursue their narrow interests at the expense of others.[15]

Another recurring theme in Catholic teaching is the importance of the growing body of international law emerging from the work of these institutions. Paul VI urges "respect for international law." And Benedict XVI argues that "a global juridic culture" requires "international norms." He writes, "It bears repeating: power must always be disciplined by law, and this applies also to relations between sovereign States." Indeed, just as political power within nations must be exercised according to the rule of law, the Vatican is clear that "political authority exercised at the level of the international community must be regulated by law" as well.[16] As within nations, the rule of law makes it easier for parties in a conflict to avoid violence. John Paul II contrasts "the law of force" with the "force of law" and states, "Peace and international law are closely linked to each other: law favors peace." From charters such as the Universal Declaration of Human Rights to institutions such as the International Court of Justice, Catholic teaching consistently emphasizes the link between international law and efforts on behalf of a more humane and less violent world.[17]

Both the Universal Declaration of Human Rights and the International Court of Justice were established by the United Nations, the most prominent of the world's intergovernmental organizations, and one the Vatican strongly endorses, though while also urging reforms to improve its contributions to global governance.[18] While urging the UN to become more efficient and share power more fairly within the organization—to "offer all its Member States an equal opportunity to be part of the decision-making process, eliminating privileges and discriminations which weaken its role and its credibility"—church statements nonetheless praise the organization for being an "effective" agent of "solidarity and peace" and "an obligatory reference point of justice and a channel of peace." Francis writes, "There is a need to prevent this Organization from being delegitimized, since its problems and shortcomings are capable of being jointly addressed and resolved." And John Paul II writes: "It must be acknowledged, however, that the United Nations Organization, even with limitations and delays due in great part to the failures of its members, has made a notable contribution to the promotion of respect for human dignity, the freedom of peoples and the requirements of development, thus preparing the cultural and institutional soil for the building of peace."[19]

— In the infrastructure of global governance established by the growing web of international treaties, laws, intergovernmental organizations, and civil society groups, Catholic teaching sees "a system capable" of "securing disarmament and settling conflicts by peaceful methods."[20]

On disarmament, the church has long advocated, in the words of Benedict XVI, "concrete agreements aimed at an effective demilitarization." This requires treaties reducing arms stockpiles, banning certain classes of arms entirely (landmines, cluster bombs, and nuclear, biological, and chemical weapons), and eliminating the sale and transfer of weapons since "arms can never in any way be treated like other goods exchanged on the world or internal market." Francis even proposes that "with the money spent on weapons and other military expenditures, let us establish a global fund that can finally put an end to hunger and favor development in the most impoverished countries so their citizens will not resort to violence or illusionary solutions."[21]

On peaceful alternatives to war, the Vatican has long argued that "it is absolutely necessary that international conflicts should not be settled by war, but that other methods better befitting human nature should be found." The more the international community develops mutual trust and cooperates to address common global problems, the more likely its participants are to turn to dialogue rather than arms to resolve disputes, creating a norm against resorting to military force. This is why the Vatican frequently urges that international laws and organizations include structures to promote, as Francis puts it in *Fratelli Tutti*, "tireless recourse to negotiation, mediation, and arbitration" for conflicts both within and between countries. For John Paul II, "reliable procedures for the resolution of conflicts" are critical to building peace, especially in areas of the world with chronic armed conflict, where international assistance to help end existing wars through cease-fires and peace agreements, and then prevent recurrences, is crucial to the regional "consolidation of peace." In such conflict zones, involving both state and nonstate actors, Benedict XVI praises peace agreements that combine diplomatic negotiation by political leaders with "grass-roots peace-making" by ordinary activists and citizens as especially vital.[22]

GLOBAL GOVERNANCE

Countries once routinely went to war to collect debts. Seizing territory and other assets to pay money owed to a state or its citizens by another state or its citizens was considered normal and legitimate; it seemed obviously necessary to ensure borrowers didn't cheat their creditors. Yet, as the political scientist Martha Finnemore details, "the practice stopped in the early twentieth century," and no country "even considers using force to collect debts anymore." Why? She concludes that the explanation does not lie in any shifts in material power among states. Instead, it was a shift in norms and the rise of alternatives. New international laws and institutions provided a different way to view disputes over debts and to resolve them. As these "came to be perceived by states as both morally superior and more useful than military solutions," wars to collect debts lost legitimacy. Eventually states internalized the norm against them to the point where they no longer even contemplate launching one.[23]

For Finnemore and other international relations scholars, this illustrates a key reality in the way countries interact in the world. It is not the unrestrained struggle of material power and sheer force that people sometimes imagine. States do act on self-interest, but how they understand their self-interest and how they understand ways to pursue it do not appear out of thin air. As with individuals, states exist in a context shaped by particular cultural meanings, norms, and institutions. This influences how states define themselves, their interests, and the options open to them. It shapes how they perceive the identity and actions of other states. As Alexander Wendt puts it, "The character of international life is determined by the beliefs and expectations that states have about each other." Over time, these beliefs and expectations become institutionalized, determining the routine ways countries interact, shaping what counts as common sense or realistic behavior in given situations. Certain ways of doing things become simply "taken for granted rather than objects of calculation."[24]

Now, this doesn't automatically lead to more peaceful coexistence. At some points in history, the institutionalized norms and expectations countries share—how they view their interests, each other, their options—push them toward frequent warfare (over debt collection, for instance). But it can work the other way too, pushing state behavior in the direction Catholic teaching urges, toward more cooperative interactions that avoid armed force (not fighting wars to collect debts, for instance). Furthermore, as Finnemore shows, intentionally shifting norms and expectations is possible. When "actors consciously set out to change the perceptions and values of others," to alter "the normative fabric of world politics," they don't always succeed, but sometimes they do. Patient efforts to create new international laws and institutions, ones that embody new norms, have, over time, shifted "views of the world and of the legitimacy or efficacy of force."[25] There is nothing inevitable in how often and for what reasons countries go to war. Therefore, shaping their behavior in order to prevent it is possible.

— Fortunately, this has become easier over the last century with the emergence of the stronger infrastructure for global governance that Catholic teaching supports. Since World War II, the international community has developed a thick network of intergovernmental organizations, treaty-based bodies, and formal diplomatic forums. At the same time, the number of internationally focused nongovernmental organizations, foundations, and grassroots civil society groups has risen dramatically. This decentralized but overlapping web of institutions and actors provides the basis for ongoing transnational negotiation and cooperation on a diverse array of issues.[26]

Where can we see this at work? In the countless shipping containers and bank transactions constantly moving around the world every second. In routine extraditions of fugitives. In negotiated catch-limits in international fisheries. In coordinated actions to address counterfeiting, smuggling, piracy, and other transnational crimes. In the way scientists track infectious diseases. In global sports tournaments such as the World Cup or the Olympics. In protections for endangered species. In international student exchanges. In the taken-for-granted global delivery of mail. In thousands of flights moving into, out of, and over countries each day. In limits on ozone-depleting chemicals. In seabed exploration rules in international waters. The list could go on and on.

None of this is to say that such efforts are always smooth or fair or effective; they have plenty of flaws, and sometimes they break down. But, on balance, they do build greater predictability and reciprocity into how members of the international community interact with each other. These institutions also don't eliminate self-interest, disputes, and even attempts to cheat. They are, however, designed to handle such things by accommodating ongoing bargaining and monitoring compliance.

Perhaps most significantly, these institutions still exercise political power. They bring pressure on parties to join up in the first place and then to follow the rules once they're in. This can include positive incentives such as favorable trade arrangements, development aid, technology transfers, diplomatic recognition, debt relief, or seats on international or regional bodies. But it can also include negative sanctions such as higher tariffs, blocking financial transactions, freezing assets, embargoing targeted goods, travel bans, cutting the flow of luxury items consumed by elites, international court indictments, or expulsion from sports competitions, cultural institutions, or intergovernmental organizations. These various inducements and penalties form a toolbox of methods that members of the international community can now use to try to shape each other's actions. They are not always successful, but they can be powerful motivators and often do change the behavior of state and nonstate actors alike.[27]

What is interesting is that even when these institutions facilitating global governance don't directly address armed conflict—but instead matters such as travel, pollution, trade, or others—participating in them still reduces the odds a country will experience war. Merely belonging to intergovernmental bodies and, to a lesser extent, trade organizations seems to make countries less warlike. They foster the kind of regular contact, information sharing, and negotiation that build trust and reciprocity. Participants are more likely to see each other as partners, even if adversarial ones, rather than enemies. Political, social, and economic integration creates shared stakes in keeping the peace. All this lowers, even if it doesn't entirely eliminate, the risk of warfare within and between states. In their review of the literature on armed conflict, David Cortright, Conor Seyle, and Kristen Wall conclude that "multilateral institutions help build peaceful relations among and within participating states" and that "global economic integration helps promote peace."[28]

PREVENTING WAR

Aside from these indirect effects, how can greater global governance more directly reduce armed conflict?

One way uses the same methods the world relies upon to manage trade or public health or mail delivery to coordinate nonmilitary responses to shared security threats. Take international terrorism, for example. Almost all those who study terrorist groups agree that war is an especially ineffective way to combat them. As a form of "asymmetrical warfare," terrorist tactics are specifically designed to thwart militarily superior opponents. Terrorists see themselves as soldiers in a righteous cause, so giving them a war is exactly what they want in order to validate their cause. And warfare also tends to make the local population they claim to represent suffer even more, often driving up support for the terrorist cause and bringing in new recruits. For instance, studies show that over 95 percent of suicide bombings are motivated by military occupations of disputed homelands. In their book *How Terrorist Groups End*, Seth Jones and Martin Libicki sum up the consensus view: "Our analysis suggests that there is no battlefield solution to terrorism. Military force usually has the opposite effect from what is intended."[29]

Aside from addressing the underlying political and economic conditions that give rise to terrorist groups in the first place, which we will consider in the next chapter, a much more effective strategy for combating such groups is transnational law enforcement. This approach treats terrorists as criminals rather than giving them the war they seek. It is also less likely to alienate local populations with military occupations, drone strikes, and the like. Furthermore, it targets a crucial weakness in most terrorist groups: they are simultaneously criminal organizations, ones almost always operating across international borders. In order to plan and carry out attacks, they need to engage in actions such as smuggling, money laundering, forging documents, illegal border crossings, and tax evasion. Many secure the funds they need through fraud, counterfeiting, robbery, kidnapping, extortion, and other crimes. This makes them vulnerable to actions by national and international law enforcement agencies working together to infiltrate, disrupt, and cut off the resources they need to operate. In his research, Mark Hamm finds that such criminal justice approaches are "the most successful method of both detecting and prosecuting cases of terrorism." International terrorism is a global security challenge that crosses borders, and the best response, far more effective than war, is law enforcement collaboration that also crosses borders.[30]

Arms control is another area of international cooperation, and one particularly prominent in Catholic teaching. As we saw in the last chapter, arms buildups increase the odds war will break out when other risk factors are also present. After wars end, arms also increase the risk countries will relapse; Cortright, Seyle, and Wall write, "Research shows that countries maintaining large armed forces in the wake of armed conflict are more likely to experience renewed armed conflict."[31] Some types of weapons, such as landmines and cluster munitions, are also especially dangerous to noncombatants. And, of course, nuclear and biological weapons have such lethal power that any instance of their use is potentially catastrophic (even if—again, as we saw in the last chapter—there is some evidence that the devastating power of nuclear weapons may make some countries less likely to go to war). All this adds up to a host of shared security concerns for the international community that are created by the flow of weapons around the world. Regulating and reducing that flow should therefore be a global priority.

Fortunately, history shows that countries can negotiate and successfully implement arms control treaties. There is evidence that the norm against using weapons of mass destruction has helped limit their spread. A significant number of countries, for example, that have the capacity to develop nuclear weapons have either declined to do so or actually given up active programs. A growing number of countries have also endorsed international treaties banning landmines and cluster munitions, though major military powers such as the United States, China, and Russia are not yet among them. There is still a long way to go; the arms trade overall remains one of the most corrupt and least regulated on earth, subject to fewer controls, for instance, than the trade in bananas. But the international community does have the tools to do much more.[32]

— Another way greater global governance can reduce armed conflict is targeting it directly through international law. In *The Internationalists*, their groundbreaking history of warfare and international law over the last century, Oona Hathaway and Scott Shapiro provide a powerful account of this process. Their story begins with how countries understood warfare and its role in the roughly three hundred years leading up to the early twentieth century. War was a legitimate and ordinary part of the international system: "States could not imagine doing without it." It was the primary method they used to resolve differences and punish perceived wrongs. Conquering territories through war conferred a legal right to rule them, and countries considered armed conquest a valid tool to acquire colonies, force favorable trade agreements, collect debts, punish treaty violations, uphold alliances, maintain a balance of power, defend or spread a particular religion, enforce hereditary succession laws, and achieve a variety of other purposes, many of which "today would be deemed utterly absurd, but which were then deemed entirely legitimate." Interestingly, the rules were clear that countries not party to an armed conflict must stay strictly neutral; even showing trade favoritism toward one side or the other made them "co-belligerents" and justified punitive attacks on them. This "precluded the possibility of economic sanctions," meaning one of the very things that would later become a key alternative to war was once considered a justification for it. Hathaway and Shapiro sum up this older international order, writing, "Resorting to arms did not signal a failure of the system: It was how the system worked."[33]

The effect of such a system, of course, was lots of wars and violent transfers of territory. After World War I made the system's costs especially apparent, and this time for colonial powers rather than just their colonies, the "internationalists" of the book's title set out to transform it. Recall Finnemore's claim, in the last section of this chapter, that with persistent effort, actors can gradually shift international norms and institutions, thereby changing state behavior. Hathaway and Shapiro detail an example of this in action, focusing on the political leaders, diplomats, and lawyers—most largely forgotten today—who worked to "replace one international order with another." Their goal was to delegitimize war between states by declaring it a crime under international law, and their patient diplomatic work eventually produced the 1928 Paris Peace Pact (known in the US as the Kellogg-Briand Pact). This agreement committed its parties, in its words, to "condemn recourse to war for the solution of international controversies, and renounce it, as an instrument of national policy in their relations with each other." It was signed by the majority of the world's countries at the time, though most interpreted it as outlawing only wars of aggression, while still permitting self-defensive ones, conducted in response to attack.[34]

In the short term, the Peace Pact seemed a spectacular failure, since just over a decade later all its signatories, except Ireland, were fighting in World War II. But for Hathaway and Shapiro, the agreement marked "the beginning of a transformation, not the end." Its initial problem was that in disavowing war, it rejected the only widely accepted tool to resolve international disputes and enforce treaties such as the pact itself, a dilemma that also undermined the League of Nations during the same period. Merely renouncing war was not enough. It was also necessary to replace its role in the international system with alternatives, and it was only several decades later, after World War II's end, that this began happening. As the international community developed the thick web of global governance institutions we saw in the last section, it acquired nonmilitary tools to resolve conflicts and influence state behavior, a process that "reaffirmed, consolidated, and institutionalized the transformation that began in 1928."[35]

For Hathaway and Shapiro, the Peace Pact's norm against war and the enforcement toolbox that emerged after World War II amount to one of "the most transformative events of human history, one that has, ultimately, made our world far more peaceful." The most remarkable impact is the collapse of wars of territorial conquest—annexing lands, redrawing international borders, carving out colonies, and the like. It still happens, as the 2022 Russian invasion of Ukraine shows, but, they argue, "we need to step back from the current headlines to look at how state behavior has changed" dramatically in this area. Such wars used to be common—standard operating procedure for countries—but now they are rare exceptions, which is why they are so shocking when they do happen. The world has gone from where an average country could "expect to lose territory in a conquest once in an ordinary human lifetime" to now only between one and two times every thousand years. The size of territory taken in wars of aggression is also a fraction of what it once was. And, perhaps most remarkable, almost all territory seized by armed conquest since the Peace Pact's signing in 1928 has ended up being returned. It became much more difficult to get conquests to "stick" once the international community shifted from thinking they conferred a legal right to rule to considering them illegal and illegitimate.[36]

— In examining how the international community first created new norms against wars of conquest and then found ways to enforce them, Hathaway and Shapiro turn to the legal concept of "outcasting." This is a crucial way groups enforce their rules. Being part of a group—from a hunter-gatherer band to an international trade organization—brings mutual benefits that create incentives to stay in the group and follow its rules. Breaking the rules risks being cast out, losing those mutual benefits and facing penalties instead—searching for food alone or facing higher tariffs and more trade restrictions compared to other countries. According to Hathaway and Shapiro, the world's many international organizations now provide lots of outcasting opportunities to either incentivize or punish countries, thereby influencing the actions they take.[37]

This fits with what other scholars have discovered about how the international community can act to prevent war. Whereas armed force was once the dominant tool states used to restrain each other's behavior, they can now deploy the full set of nonmilitary incentives and sanctions associated with the infrastructure of global governance. Although they are not guaranteed to succeed, the evidence indicates that these can be effective in pushing countries toward less warlike behavior. They are especially powerful if sanctions are targeted as specifically as possible toward a country's leaders and other elites rather than ordinary citizens, if sanctions are also packaged with positive incentives that provide off-ramps for war, if these come from a broad coalition of other countries rather than only one or a few, and if the goal of such pressure is not complete regime change, which can cause leaders in the target country to dig in, but rather more modest shifts in the regime's actions away from armed force. Furthermore, this pressure is best used not merely to punish a country as an end in itself, but instead as leverage to push it into international structures that facilitate negotiation and nonmilitary dispute resolution. A diverse combination of targeted rewards and punishments can bring states to the bargaining table and shift them toward war's alternatives.[38] As Matthew Levinger writes, "For international actors seeking to prevent deadly conflict, it is essential to shift decision makers' strategic calculus by decreasing the relative benefits and increasing the relative costs of resorting to violence."[39]

Sometimes pushing adversaries into one-on-one dialogue is enough. In *How Enemies Become Friends*, Charles Kupchan demonstrates that ongoing diplomatic exchanges between countries that were once armed opponents can, over time, transform their relationship into one of peaceful coexistence.[40] Often, however, third parties play crucial roles in helping opponents, both states and substate armed groups, engage in a process of conflict resolution and prevention. These third parties can be other countries, groups of countries, or regional and global intergovernmental bodies. They can also be nonstate groups—as when Swiss and Finnish nongovernmental organizations mediated talks between the Indonesian government and secessionists in the Aceh Province in 2003 and 2005—and religious organizations and leaders—which have helped resolve conflicts from Mozambique to India to Sudan to Northern Ireland. John Paul II himself successfully mediated a border dispute between Argentina and Chile early in his papacy.[41]

Institutions and individuals specializing in conflict prevention and resolution study factors that make escalation to warfare more likely. They monitor early warning signs, since, as in medicine, earlier interventions are usually more successful, as when the UN acted soon enough to mediate a brewing dispute between Greece and North Macedonia following the latter's independence from Yugoslavia in the 1990s, with the result that the dispute was eventually resolved with the Prespa Agreement.[42] Skilled mediators are able to use a range of techniques—sharing information, confidence-building actions, security guarantees, verifying that parties have taken agreed-upon steps—to reduce uncertainty and distrust, change perceptions of a conflict, reframe the range of options open to parties, and provide face-saving measures on the path to settlement. Success is by no means guaranteed, but these efforts have accumulated an impressive record of effectiveness.[43] An even more formal approach involves arbitration by an official global body or court acting under international law, where decisions are binding on parties. This method has been especially successful in border disputes, as when in 2002 the International Court of Justice awarded Cameroon a disputed oil-rich region, and Nigeria, a militarily more powerful neighbor that also claimed it, pulled its troops out and respected the ruling.[44]

The presence of widespread opportunities for mediation and arbitration has reduced the extent to which countries automatically look to armed force to protect their interests and resolve disputes. While certainly not universal, these alternatives have become much more common, especially for countries that are not major powers. But their success often remains hidden compared to when wars break out and the world takes notice. As Joshua Goldstein observes, the reason they "do not get more attention is precisely that they were successful—there was no war."[45]

— It is important to realize that nonmilitary ways to interact and resolve differences are the norm among countries, while warfare is the exception. The cooperation Catholic teaching urges is actually pretty common, and the standard response to disputes is bargaining and compromise. Most countries are not at war most of the time. Many haven't experienced it for generations, and some not for centuries. This is not because they don't experience disputes with neighbors, trading partners, and others. It's just that they use methods other than war to address them. As Christopher Blattman puts it, "For every war that ever was, a thousand others have been averted through discussion and concession." And, echoing language often used by the Vatican, the military historian John Keegan writes, "It is the spirit of cooperativeness, not confrontation, that makes the world go round."[46]

War still exists, of course, but as more alternatives have emerged with the international community's greater capacity for global governance over the last century, it has suffered a decline in legitimacy. Most countries, though still not all, now see war as an exceptional measure at best, not a normal tool of statecraft. This is particularly evident in the shift we saw Hathaway and Shapiro detail in *The Internationalists*. The decline of wars to conquer new territory and colonies—which results, in turn, in fewer wars seeking to liberate those territories and overthrow those colonizers—has been especially significant, because territorial disputes are historically more likely to escalate into war than other types. A stronger norm against such wars and more nonmilitary alternatives to handle territorial disputes have had a huge impact on the international system. Indeed, it is one of the key drivers in an overall decline of warfare between countries that we will examine more closely in chapter 5.[47]

A significant number of countries now exist in zones of the world where war is essentially off the table. Where disputes, whether over territory, trade, ideology, resources, or other matters, are handled nonmilitarily as a matter of course. Where countries with more powerful militaries don't even think of invading their weaker neighbors, even resource-rich ones. That is not to say such areas don't have plenty of problems, including other forms of political violence. Only that large numbers of countries manage to interact and regularly resolve differences without ever considering a resort to warfare.[48]

We can draw two conclusions from all this. First, institutions facilitating global governance can and do prevent armed conflict. The tools Catholic teaching emphasizes provide effective alternatives to war. Second, the church is also correct that this process is incomplete. Because there is still plenty of warfare, there is still plenty of work to do. It is possible to build on global governance's success by further strengthening its infrastructure and refining its methods, especially as we learn more about which ones are most effective.[49]

AREAS OF PERSISTENT ARMED CONFLICT

Just as some parts of the world are zones largely free of war, other regions or countries experience high levels of armed conflict. Examples include Yemen, eastern Ukraine, the Horn of Africa, and Afghanistan. Warfare, then, is not spread evenly across the globe. But this distribution is not inevitable. All the world's more peaceful regions where once warlike, so it is possible that those currently plagued by war can also move in a more peaceful direction. Efforts to strengthen global governance and its ability to prevent war are most pressing in these regions.

Most wars in the world today are civil wars within states, including ones that spill across borders and pull other countries into overlapping domestic conflicts. These wars also tend to confirm Catholic teaching's emphasis on cycles of violence; they are frequently chronic stop-and-start conflicts, going through periods of more intense combat, interrupted by intermittent suspensions in fighting, only to see conflicts restart again, often spreading in new directions. The majority of civil wars are actually relapses of previous ones, and once a civil war ends, it has strong odds of starting up again within a few years.[50]

As we saw in the last chapter, intervening militarily in active civil wars tends to only prolong them. A better approach is to use sources of nonmilitary leverage to push parties toward pauses in the fighting, and then use these intervals to help prevent relapses and support local populations in efforts to build a more durable peace. Helping break cycles of persistent, recurring war in regions that experience it most frequently is the most promising short-term way to reduce the volume of warfare around the world.

— This process begins by pressuring parties to institute cease-fires and open negotiations. For example, after a decade of civil war between the government of Nepal and armed Maoist insurgents, a combination of domestic civil resistance and pressure on the Nepalese government by

India, its more powerful neighbor, forced the government to open peace negotiations; the result was a 2004 comprehensive peace settlement that ended the conflict and ushered in democratic reforms.[51] Research shows that the international community can effectively use its toolbox of incentives and sanctions to bring governments and armed groups to the bargaining table, ending civil wars much sooner than letting them run their course. Even seemingly intractable civil wars are not immune to outside pressure.[52]

It is not enough to just end the fighting. Negotiated settlements are crucial. While they can and do break down, they have a better record of securing lasting peace than other possible outcomes, such as cease-fires alone or even outright victory by one side. They also work best in combination with outside peacekeeping initiatives. Parties to a conflict are more likely to negotiate and sign peace agreements if third-party peacekeepers provide security guarantees, and, in turn, peacekeeping is most successful in combination with such agreements. Peacekeeping operations that enter during periods of active fighting are more likely to fail than those that enter in the context of cease-fires and negotiated settlements. In their influential study of peacekeeping, Michael Doyle and Nicholas Sambanis argue that this timing is critical to increasing the odds that peacekeeping will successfully build the "capacity for self-sustaining peace."[53]

Cease-fires, negotiated settlements, and postconflict peacekeeping are a much more successful formula for ending civil wars and avoiding restarts than military interventions. Comprehensive peacekeeping operations, especially under the auspices of the UN, can be especially effective in breaking cycles of violence and preventing countries from slipping back into armed conflict. Indeed, the presence of third-party peacekeepers reduces the risk of relapse to war by over half.[54] In the immediate wake of armed conflicts, especially civil wars, parties who have until recently been trying to kill each other are understandably mistrustful; they don't know if the other side is acting in good faith and upholding its commitments, or if it is cheating and preparing to launch new attacks. Third-party peacekeepers help agreements stick by addressing these security dilemmas. They monitor deals, verify actions such as disarmament or withdrawal from particular areas, head off spoilers, and enable ongoing communication. They can begin facilitating the arrival of humanitarian and economic aid or the return of refugees in even-handed ways. And they can help provide security and restore government services.[55]

This last element is especially important since stop-and-start armed conflict is more likely in conditions of weak governance. Many contemporary civil wars feature what John Mueller calls "opportunistic predation." Combatants engage in plunder, extortion, and smuggling as much as combat. Warlords, militias, mercenaries, and government troops can all profit from the lawlessness and organized crime that thrive in war zones. In countries such as Colombia, Angola, and the Democratic Republic of Congo, civil wars have been prolonged by the illegal trade in drugs or minerals. This is why neutral third parties can begin to reestablish order, security, the rule of law, and basic government services in ways that help prevent a country from relapsing into war.[56]

So while peacekeeping initiatives don't always work, they do more often than most people realize, significantly increasing the chances for durable peace. Praising the "unarmy" of mediators, aid workers, and humanitarian groups, Goldstein concludes, "Considering how few funds and resources they get, these international peace operations have succeeded remarkably well."[57] There is, however, significant room for improvement. Better planning and coordination, expanded institutional capacity, quicker deployments, and slower drawdowns can all make peacekeeping operations more effective. More successful than war in bringing peace, they nonetheless get a fraction of the planning and resources, so reversing that ratio holds great promise. The average US household, for instance, contributes 350 times as many tax dollars to military operations as to peacekeeping ones.[58]

— To increase its odds of success, the cease-fire-agreement-peacekeeping formula cannot deal only with armed combatants; it has to include broad-based representation from local civilian populations as well. For instance, Maria Stephan writes, "Multiple studies have found that women's inclusion in peace processes correlates significantly with their success." In her research, Marie O'Reilly finds that when women and women's groups are part of negotiated agreements to end armed conflicts, such agreements are more likely to be reached, to be implemented, and to have enduring success, thus boosting effectiveness each step of the way. She concludes that women are more trusted mediators, more skilled at depolarizing negotiations and building bridges, more likely to include a wider array of relevant issues, and more likely to prioritize postconflict gender equity, which, as we will see in the next chapter, itself lowers the risk of future armed conflict.[59]

Similarly, including local peace groups and other civil society organizations boosts the odds that a peace process will succeed. Such groups bring in a wider range of voices, facilitating communication, building bridges, and including a broader range of pertinent issues. As Cortright, Seyle, and Wall state, "The risk of renewed armed conflict falls by 50 percent when civil society is at the negotiating table."[60]

Even in active war zones, most people do not participate in armed conflict. They find ways, including nonviolent civil resistance methods, to avoid being dragged into the war. Such people, their movements, and their communities are additional resources for peacekeepers working to break cycles of warfare, since they are well equipped to keep up grassroots pressure for peaceful progress, facilitate nonviolent negotiation, and promote reconciliation.[61]

— There is one more important dimension to note here. International efforts to reduce war in parts of the world where its risks are greatest are also the best way to prevent mass atrocities, including genocide. As we have seen, these atrocities rarely happen without a war already underway, so breaking cycles of violent conflict simultaneously reduces their risk too. But it is also possible to target mass atrocities specifically during such efforts.

Since mass atrocities do not happen instantly and spontaneously, but instead escalate over time and require planning and coordination, scholars have identified early warning signs. Underlying political, social, and economic factors, as well as specific shifts in the rhetoric and actions of a country's leaders, can signal elevated risk for mass atrocities.[62] This allows for early interventions using many of the same tools for heading off wars, bringing diplomatic and economic pressure to bear on leaders to change course and channel disputes in directions less likely to produce mass violence, a strategy that has proven effective. Blocking the influx of weapons into target countries can also help, as can stopping the outflow of valuable resources (diamonds, oil, coltan, tin, timber) controlled by governments or armed militias.[63] Owen Pell and Kelly Bonner also point out that multinational corporations operating in conflict zones have significant economic leverage over local business elites and political leaders, so international regulations that require and incentivize these corporations to adopt atrocity prevention strategies that use this leverage have significant promise.[64]

As in preventing war more generally, nonmilitary international efforts to prevent mass atrocities have proven effective, though the fact that they are not always successful means there is more work to do.

— We can see, then, that Catholic teaching's case for preventing war through greater global governance is strongly supported by the evidence on armed conflict. This does not require removing self-interest, conflict, or power from international politics. Instead, these can be effectively channeled into global institutional networks that provide alternative sets of norms, dispute-resolution mechanisms, and tools to shape behavior and facilitate cooperation, just as the Vatican urges.

We now turn to the church's longer-term focus on preventing war by removing its underlying economic, social, and political roots.

CHAPTER 4

PREVENTING WAR THROUGH ECONOMIC AND POLITICAL JUSTICE

Alongside greater global governance, the other area of emphasis in Catholic teaching's comprehensive strategy for preventing war is a deeper and longer-term project. For the church, it is imperative that humanity address the underlying conditions that cause war in the first place. This means sustained, multidimensional work on behalf of a more just world.

The best place to start is with Catholic teaching's understanding of peace. Vatican documents regularly state that "peace is not merely the absence of war" but is instead, in the words of the Second Vatican Council, "rightly and appropriately called an enterprise of justice." According to *Gaudium et Spes*, to prevent wars, it is vital to "build up peace," and doing so means "the causes of discord among men, especially injustice, which foment wars must be rooted out." Paul VI advocates an antiwar vision that "grounds peace in justice, both in relations between nations and in relations within each nation." As he succinctly puts it in his most famous formulation: "If you want peace, work for justice."[1]

Since Vatican II, advocating for a more just, and therefore more peaceful, world has been central to Catholic teaching. The 1971 World

Synod of Catholic Bishops calls "action on behalf of justice and participation in the transformation of the world" a "constitutive dimension" of the mission of the church. A more just and peaceful world won't happen on its own. It is "a great political project," as Francis calls it, one necessitating comprehensive global action. The church, then, sees itself as a voice demanding political efforts on behalf of systematic and structural justice. In *Evangelii Nuntiandi*, Paul VI points to the need to "build up structures which are more human, more just, more respective of the rights of the person and less oppressive." The Second Vatican Council calls such efforts "setting up the instruments of peace."[2]

In articulating what a more just and peaceful world looks like, Vatican statements envision one that avoids violence, coercion, political oppression, and economic inequality and exploitation. Instead, it promotes human dignity, rights, and cooperation. It provides all persons and groups the resources necessary to flourish and the ability to participate in the political decisions that shape their lives. In short, it is one that upholds the global common good.[3] As the Second Vatican Council writes:

> Every day human interdependence grows more tightly drawn and spreads by degrees over the whole world. As a result the common good, that is, the sum of those conditions of social life which allow social groups and their individual members relatively thorough and ready access to their own fulfillment, today takes on an increasingly universal complexion and consequently involves rights and duties with respect to the whole human race. Every social group must take account of the needs and legitimate aspirations of other groups, and even of the general welfare of the entire human family.[4]

Both Paul VI and Benedict XVI point out, however, that just institutions and structures are not enough. They go hand in hand with cultivating a "culture and ethos" that promotes certain norms and virtues, ones such as collaboration, mutual aid, reconciliation, forgiveness, and respect. Perhaps the most important of these is the virtue of solidarity, that special commitment to the common good and dignity of all. In *Sollicitudo rei Socialis*, John Paul II calls peace "the fruit of solidarity." And Francis writes: "Solidarity means much more than engaging in sporadic acts of generosity. It means thinking and acting in terms of community. It means that the lives of all are prior to the appropriation of goods by a few. It also means combatting the structural causes of poverty, inequality, the lack of work, land and housing, the denial of social and labour rights."[5]

— So, according to the church, preventing war means actively building justice and peace. More justice and peace, in turn, prevents war, creating a virtuous cycle—the very opposite of the vicious cycle of violence, injustice, and insecurity that war itself creates. Nurturing the virtuous version of this cycle requires political action at multiple levels—internationally, nationally, regionally, and locally—by both government and nongovernment actors. For Catholic teaching, such action attacks the roots of war itself. By working for economic, social, and political changes that increase global justice, it prevents wars by eliminating the conditions that breed them. In *Centesimus Annus*, John Paul II writes: "Furthermore, it must not be forgotten that at the root of war there are usually real and serious grievances: injustices suffered, legitimate aspirations frustrated, poverty, and the exploitation of multitudes of desperate people who see no real possibility of improving their lot by peaceful means." Benedict XVI points to "the underlying reasons for conflicts, often provoked by injustice." And Francis sees the origins of war in the "indifference to others and their dignity" that produces political oppression, economic exploitation, powerlessness, environmental destruction, and denial of "elementary rights, such as the right to food, water, healthcare or employment." Such conditions "risk exploding sooner or later into acts of violence and insecurity" as people who have been denied "basic rights and needs" are "tempted to obtain them by force."[6]

Eliminating the roots of war begins with economic development, which Paul VI calls "the new name for peace."[7] Francis writes, "There can be no true peace unless we show ourselves capable of developing a more just economic system." The Vatican regularly condemns "the miseries of underdevelopment" such as hunger, disease, joblessness, debt bondage, harsh and unsafe working conditions, and a lack of access to shelter, healthcare, or education. For John Paul II, "conditions of extreme poverty," caused by "an unjust distribution of resources between peoples and between social classes" and by separating persons "from their rightful access to the goods meant for all," are manifestly immoral and a "grave threat to peace." Poverty is both a cause and a consequence of war. John Paul II further argues that conditions of extreme poverty are even more troubling when contrasted with the extravagant "super-development" of others. Catholic teaching considers the widening gap between rich and poor, both between and within countries, a violation of solidarity and a source of "tension and conflict" that undermines "the establishment of stable conditions for authentic peace."[8]

The proper response is concerted worldwide action to address both extreme poverty and inequality, working toward "a world that is more just and prosperous for all," in John Paul II's words. He points out that economic development is not an automatic process that happens on its own. The obstacles are less economic than political: "Just as within individual societies it is possible and right to organize a solid economy which will direct the functioning of the market to the common good, so too there is a similar need for adequate interventions on the international level" by "effective international agencies." For Benedict XVI, writing in *Caritas in Veritate*, "the integrated economy of the present day does not make the role of States redundant, but rather it commits governments to greater collaboration with one another." These efforts, if properly "directed, open up the unprecedented possibility of large-scale redistribution of wealth on a world-wide scale."[9] Since, as Francis puts it, "the lives of all are prior to the appropriation of goods by a few," a more equitable distribution of resources will make sure all can live lives of dignity. This means robust development efforts should target (to cite some of the priorities frequently invoked by the Vatican) land reform; access to capital; universal education, especially for girls; worker cooperatives, unions, and access to jobs with a living wage; retirement pensions; universal healthcare coverage; and debt relief and protections against predatory lending.[10]

Catholic teaching considers development efforts a responsibility of the entire globe, saying "either all the nations of the world participate, or it will not be true development." Even more important is the greater responsibility of wealthy and powerful nations to contribute more. John Paul II, for instance, demands "a concerted worldwide effort to promote development, an effort which also involves sacrificing the positions of income and power enjoyed by the more developed economies." Benedict XVI warns that development should never be a way the powerful—whether companies, nations, or groups—manipulate "peoples and countries which have little weight in the international market." It should be an equitable, participatory process that "gives poorer nations an effective voice in shared decision-making." In particular, "free trade" should not be a tool to increase inequality, undermine social safety nets, or reduce worker rights. The church also warns against development assistance being siphoned off by corrupt officials before reaching those in need, endorsing careful monitoring, accountability, and directing aid through grassroots civil society groups as well.[11]

As awareness of threats to the earth's environment has grown from the mid-twentieth century, Catholic teaching has increasingly addressed what John Paul II calls the "ecological crisis," incorporating sustainability into its teaching on economic development. The Vatican condemns climate change, resource depletion, pollution, and other environmental harms as attacks on the global common good, ones with particularly harsh impacts on the world's poor. Indeed, in *Evangelium Vitae*, John Paul II calls "reckless tampering with the world's ecological balance" a form of violence. Francis warns that war harms the environment, even as environmental stress means "the scene will be set for new wars." And

Benedict XVI states, "If you want to cultivate peace, protect creation." Since doing so "entails a shared responsibility for all humanity," coordinated global environmental action is critical to justice and peace, and so it should be woven into every dimension of economic development.[12]

— Economic development, however, is not enough to fully address the roots of war. The Vatican's understanding of development, which it calls "integral" or "authentic" development, "cannot be restricted to economic growth alone," but rather "concerns the whole of the person in every single dimension." It embraces the political, as well as economic and social, conditions that contribute to human flourishing. As Paul VI writes, "It is not just a question of eliminating hunger and reducing poverty. It is not just a question of fighting wretched conditions, though this is an urgent and necessary task. It involves building a human community where men can live truly human lives. . . . It involves building a human community where liberty is not an idle word."[13]

Like economic injustice, political injustice threatens peace. Catholic teaching condemns authoritarian, oppressive, and corrupt governments that deny basic human rights and political participation on a free and equal basis. Regimes that govern "solely or mainly by means of threats and intimidation," that use police powers to silence political dissent, that rely on concentrations of wealth, power, and privilege to prevent ordinary people, especially members of disadvantaged groups, from exercising a meaningful say over decisions that impact their lives—these all not only violate human dignity; they make violence more likely. In the words of Francis, they make it more likely that "aggression and conflict will find fertile terrain for growth and eventually explode."[14]

For the Vatican, then, "replacing dictatorial forms of government with more democratic and participatory ones" is "an indispensable component of work for peace," as John Paul II puts it. Benedict XVI also urges "the consolidation of democratic regimes capable of ensuring freedom and peace." Catholic teaching considers the common good the "sole purpose" of political authority, and the common good is best served by "truly democratic institutions," ones that sustain "democratic life and pluralism."[15]

Not all democracies take the same precise form, but healthy ones share a core set of commitments. John Paul II writes in *Centesimus Annus*, "The Church values the democratic system inasmuch as it ensures the participation of citizens in making political choices, guarantees to the governed the possibility both of electing and holding accountable those who govern them, and of replacing them through peaceful means when appropriate." Catholic teaching emphasizes openness and transparency; free, fair, and competitive elections; and widespread social participation ensured by "procedures which allow the largest possible number of citizens to participate in public affairs with genuine freedom." Political institutions should be inclusive, accountable, and based on the rule of law, since "authentic democracy is possible only in a State ruled by law." They should also be responsive to the needs of the people, with governing capacity sufficient to meet those needs. Where such institutions are lacking—due to factors such as underdevelopment, civil war, or a recent transition from autocracy—then, according to Benedict XVI, "construction or reconstruction of the State remains a key factor in their development" and a key "focus of international aid." And democracy requires that alongside state institutions there exist a free and dynamic civil society made up of "intermediary organizations" such as religious bodies, civic and advocacy groups, mutual aid societies, clubs, and other organizations.[16]

Finally, the church sees true democracy as inseparable from political and civil rights. This is one of the most common themes in modern Catholic teaching. The 1971 World Synod of Catholic Bishops states, "The right to development must be seen as the dynamic interpenetration of all those fundamental human rights upon which the aspirations of individuals and nations are based." Francis says authentic democracy is grounded in justice and "a commitment to protect the rights of every person, especially the weak and vulnerable." And Benedict XVI writes, "A true and stable peace presupposes respect for human rights." These rights include freedom of religion and conscience, association and assembly, speech and the press. They protect the ability of persons to vote, hold political office, and belong to religious bodies, civic groups, political parties, and trade unions. They guarantee the liberty to express political opinions and cultural traditions. They ensure, in the words of Paul VI in *Octogesima Adveniens*, that women have "equal rights to participate in cultural, economic, social and political life." They provide for due process in the judicial system. They protect individuals and cultural groups—especially members of vulnerable populations such as ethnic, racial, or religious minorities, migrants, or people in poverty—from abuse and discrimination. In *Pacem in Terris*, John XXIII writes, "The chief concern of civil authorities must therefore be to ensure that these rights are recognized, co-ordinated, defended and promoted." John Paul II simply states, "Peace flourishes when these rights are fully respected."[17]

INCREASING THE ODDS OF PEACE

Reducing war is both simple and difficult. The simple part is that we know what dramatically lowers the likelihood a country will experience armed conflict; it is actually the very conditions we just saw Catholic teaching emphasize in its focus on justice as the path to peace. The difficult part is supporting and spreading these conditions more broadly.

In *Governance for Peace*, their comprehensive review of armed conflict research, David Cortright, Conor Seyle, and Kristen Wall summarize what makes countries far less likely to experience war: they are marked by widely shared prosperity, openness to international trade and investment, participation in international organizations, greater gender equity, democracy and broad-based political participation, human rights protections, inclusive and accountable political institutions, and governments that deliver public services such as education, healthcare, social welfare, security, and the rule of law effectively and fairly. The authors conclude that, while complex and challenging, it is possible to move toward greater peace by strengthening these factors around the world, and they write that "sufficient evidence now exists to say with confidence that the reduction of armed conflict is possible."[18]

ECONOMIC, SOCIAL, AND ENVIRONMENTAL FACTORS

The evidence is overwhelming that certain economic conditions significantly increase the risk of war. Low-income countries with high levels of extreme poverty and unemployment are far more likely to experience armed conflicts, and these conflicts usually last longer in such countries. Economic isolation with little international trade and investment similarly raise the likelihood of warfare. And in a phenomenon known as the "resource curse," poor countries dependent on oil exports for revenue, as well as those with "lootable resources" such as diamonds or precious metals, are particularly war-prone.[19]

Inequality within a country also increases its risk for war. This is less a matter of inequality between individuals than between groups. When ethnic, religious, or regional groups face discrimination and unequal access to resources, armed conflict becomes more likely.[20] Gender inequality also increases the odds of warfare. Societies in which women experience more economic discrimination, a subordinate socioeconomic status, and lower labor-force participation are significantly more likely to be involved in both international and civil wars.[21]

In addition to these economic indicators, some closely related social factors also predict elevated risks for war. Countries whose populations suffer from poor access to healthcare, malnutrition, and high infant mortality have higher odds of armed conflict. For instance, low childhood immunization rates are directly related to higher risk of civil wars. Education access shows similar trends. Lower literacy and educational attainment rates are associated with greater chances for armed conflict. Less access to education for girls in particular elevates the risk a country will experience a civil war.[22]

What about accelerating environmental damage, which many, including the Vatican, worry makes warfare more likely? Although humans have long fought wars over natural resources, so far there is little direct evidence that environmental stress alone makes armed conflict more likely in today's world. Some case studies suggest a connection, but larger-scale research is yet to consistently confirm it. As Nils Petter Gleditsch writes, "Despite the growing concern about the consequences of environmental disruption, there is limited empirical evidence for its potential impact on armed conflict." This is not to say environmental stress won't increase the risk of war in the near future, especially if climate change and resource depletion drive up food prices, increase refugee flows, or have additional disruptive impacts that can intensify other risk factors. And, of course, Catholic teaching's call to address the "ecological crisis," especially its impact on the poor, the vulnerable, and future generations, is based on far more than its potential impact on armed conflict. But, for now at least, environmental factors remain less predictive of war than other economic and social indicators.[23]

It is important to note that just because some things are correlated with war doesn't mean they directly cause it. Low childhood immunization, for instance, is not the specific reason a particular war happens. What makes these factors important is that they indicate a set of broader and often interrelated economic and social circumstances that do seem to produce wars more often.

The good news is that it is possible to change these circumstances in order to significantly reduce war's frequency. The primary actors who can do so are within countries. These are their political and business leaders, civil society groups, religious institutions, unions, reform organizations, and professional associations. External actors can play a role too. Other countries, regional and global intergovernmental bodies, nongovernmental organizations, and humanitarian aid groups can use the global governance tools we saw at work in the last chapter to incentivize and strengthen such efforts within countries. There is, in other words, a set of strategies that those who want to reduce the odds of war, both within countries and in the broader international community, can prioritize and work toward.

— Let's start with economic development, which, Catholic teaching is correct to emphasize, is crucial to building peace. Increasing per-capita income and reducing extreme poverty is one of the most effective ways to lower a country's risk of war. This means promoting economic growth through reforms that diversify a country's economy, shifting away from overreliance on extracting raw materials such as oil or minerals. Some countries, especially in East Asia, have been successful in doing this through targeted investment in selected manufacturing/export industries. Implementing structural reforms that increase openness to trade and foreign investment is another strategy. More international trade boosts economic growth, as well as having an independent impact on reducing the likelihood of armed conflict. The development economist Marcelo Giugale, for instance, points to the huge potential of poorer African countries to deepen their trade relationships across the continent: "Only ten cents of every dollar exported from an African country goes to another African country." An important way to foster a more diversified economy with higher levels of trade is through investments in infrastructure such as ports, rail and road networks, green energy, data and communication systems, and agricultural technologies that boost productivity and reduce spoilage. Rather than high military spending, which actually lowers economic growth, these kinds of investments can increase growth in ways that reduce the odds a country will experience war—which is doubly important, since armed conflict itself sabotages efforts to increase national income and reduce extreme poverty, further increasing the risk of future war.[24]

Those who study development are careful to point out that these kinds of reforms should not be pursued as a kind of sudden "shock therapy." Markets have a critical role in economic growth, but without effective regulation, rapid market reforms can destabilize a country, increase inequality, and actually make armed conflict more likely. Instead, economic reforms designed to boost growth should be phased in gradually, evenly, and alongside investments in human capital, an effective social safety net, and regulation to avoid exploitation.[25]

Giugale argues that economic reforms that focus on ordinary people in the developing world are crucial. One example is better access to banking and credit services, combined with relatively straightforward measures that allow people to take advantage of them, such as clear legal titles to land and even identity documents like birth certificates that most people in the developed world take for granted. Another is shifting public subsidies toward those most in need. For instance, subsidized gasoline in the developing world mainly helps the small number of wealthier people who own cars. In particular, Giugale emphasizes the potential of direct cash transfers to poor citizens made possible by digital technology such as bank accounts linked to mobile phones. For people in severe poverty, even relatively small amounts of money can make a huge difference, and such transfers are a straightforward and efficient way to reduce the most extreme levels of poverty within a country, expand economic opportunity, and boost entrepreneurship. It is an approach that is proving increasingly effective.[26]

Development that reduces the likelihood of war also includes improving the lives of ordinary people when it comes to education, healthcare, and other areas of social assistance. Providing access to these basic human welfare measures is often more straightforward than increasing economic growth or trade, and countries that invest in doing so enjoy lower levels of armed conflict. Better education access is especially associated with reducing incentives for the armed rebellions that lead to civil war. Cortright, Seyle, and Wall write, "Whether measured as years of schooling, levels of public spending on education or the degree of literacy and learning in a society, educational variables are strongly associated with a greater likelihood of peace." Since military spending around the world is around ten times that of education, simply reversing that ratio could have enormous benefits in preventing war.[27]

A combination of these development actions can be especially helpful in breaking the "resource curse," where countries rich in oil or minerals are also conflict-prone. If the profits from these resources are put into building infrastructure and nurturing sectors that diversify the economy, are invested into healthcare, schools, and other social services, and paid directly to citizens as regular dividends (much as the state of Alaska does), they can do much to lessen the risk of war.[28]

— Notice a consistent theme here. Development alone is not enough. As Catholic teaching emphasizes, its benefits must be broadly shared across a society in order to most effectively contribute to peace. Giugale states that "economic development is more than a growing economy." If its benefits flow primarily to a select few, it can increase conflict and actually undermine long-term growth, since countries with wide economic inequality grow more slowly. To decrease the likelihood of war, development should reduce rather than increase inequalities between ethnic, religious, or regional groups. It should prioritize spreading prosperity, opportunity, and human welfare in equitable and inclusive ways.[29]

Development that produces greater gender equity is especially important — it is one of the single strongest predictors of peace. As Cortright, Seyle, and Wall write, "States characterized by gender equity are less likely to engage in militarized international disputes, have lower rates of military spending, and are less likely to experience internal armed conflict, repression, and human rights abuse." When women have wider opportunities, more access to education and labor markets, and lower fertility rates, war becomes less likely. Lower fertility rates provided by higher economic status, educational opportunity, and greater access to contraception have an especially strong impact on reducing the odds of war (this greater use of contraception is, of course, in tension with the Vatican's opposition to most methods of birth control). In addition to its direct association with less war, a higher socioeconomic status for women also promotes peace by contributing to growth and equality.

Countries with less labor-force and educational discrimination against women experience higher economic growth. Even relatively simple reforms can pay economic dividends. For instance, in Rwanda a land-registration system that gave women clear title to their land on an equal basis to men boosted their investment in and the productivity of their farms. And in addition to economic improvements, gender equity promotes equity more generally. One of the most powerful predictors of whether or not people experience economic and social opportunities in life is their mother's level of education. As Giugale writes, "Educating girls today enhances equity for all tomorrow."[30]

— While efforts within countries to alleviate conditions that make war more likely are crucial, these conditions have global dimensions as well. Their causes cross international borders, so their remedies should too. The entire international community has an interest in addressing these conditions (and, according to Catholic teaching, a moral responsibility to do so as well). Part of this involves the international community using its incentives/sanctions toolkit to encourage the kinds of internal reforms we just considered, but that community can also assist in more direct ways.

The Vatican is correct to emphasize the importance of foreign aid, especially increased contributions from wealthy countries, in helping to target war's roots. This does not mean, however, that all aid is automatically effective. Large, unrestricted cash infusions into a country can be captured by autocratic or corrupt leaders, bolstering their power but not producing meaningful change for ordinary citizens. Foreign assistance in building hospitals and schools is good, but it can also free up funds for domestic governments to instead buy more arms in preparation for war. Refugee camps provide help for those in need, but they can also unintentionally give militias safe havens to regroup and launch new attacks. Even large-scale humanitarian food shipments can give an armed group leverage to coerce a hungry population, or they can undermine long-term sustainable agriculture by driving local farmers out of business.[31] None of this is a reason to dismiss foreign aid completely, but instead to maximize its positive impact through better design, delivery, and grassroots partnerships.

Foreign aid is most effective when it is part of a coordinated strategy, one tailored to particular countries, targeting specific issues, and incorporating sophisticated mechanisms of accountability that help it bypass corrupt actors. It is best when phased in gradually, sustained over a longer period, and designed to fit local circumstances. Especially promising are randomized trials that identify the most effective ways to improve healthcare, education, or gender equity; programs that deliver cash assistance through local civil society groups or directly to individual recipients, rather than through national governments; and aid tied to specific benchmarks such as declines in infant mortality, increases in literacy, or reductions in military spending. The evidence is clear that well-designed aid can be an effective way to address risk factors for war by helping to reduce extreme poverty and improve human welfare.[32]

In addition to providing more foreign aid to developing countries, the world's wealthier countries can adopt their own reforms. They can reduce domestic farm subsidies to expand market opportunities for farmers in poorer countries. They can increase technology transfers that help raise economic growth in poorer regions of the world. They can more closely regulate multinational cooperations to channel a greater share of profits from resource extraction in developing countries back to their own citizens. And they can make it easier for people from developing countries to travel for work in wealthier ones, better protect them from wage theft when doing so, and make it easier for them to send back remittances, which can be an important supplement to family income in their home countries.[33]

Finally, the international community can coordinate global action in key areas. One example is debt relief. Unsustainable foreign debt burdens can hinder economic growth and investments in human welfare within developing countries. The last two decades have seen campaigns, coordinated by global and regional organizations, to successfully ease these debt burdens and help countries establish a stronger fiscal footing. Another example is global health initiatives. Since illness does not recognize borders, better funding and coordination efforts by intergovernmental and nongovernmental public health organizations to more effectively track, treat, and eliminate disease threats are crucial in improving human welfare around the world. Perhaps most challenging is global action on the environment. Resource depletion and the impacts of climate change hit those living in the developing world disproportionately hard, even as the consumption patterns in wealthier countries disproportionately cause them. And the economic growth in poorer countries that reduces the risk of war can also cause more environmental stress. It is, therefore, critical that the international community work collectively to protect natural resources and rapidly transition to renewable sources of energy. And the Vatican is correct that responsibility for such action falls more heavily on the globe's wealthier, more powerful countries.[34]

POLITICAL FACTORS

Of course, the kinds of measures reducing the odds of war that we just considered do not happen on their own. They require political action to shift resources and change policies. This is less likely to happen when governments are autocratic, corrupt, or unaccountable, or simply don't have the capacity to control their territory, deliver basic government services, or secure the rule of law. Political institutions make a big difference in whether or not peace-oriented reforms actually happen. This is why researchers, echoing Catholic teaching, emphasize the connection between economic and political development.[35]

And it turns out that political institutions have an independent impact on the likelihood of war as well. Certain political conditions make peace more likely in their own right. So whether it's their role in shaping economic or social policies or their own separate role in reducing the frequency of war more directly, a specific set of political factors is crucial to fostering peace. This is how Cortright, Seyle, and Wall summarize these factors: "Stability and peace are most assured in settings of consolidated democracy, where governing institutions enforce the rule of law and provide effective services for all, and where people are able to participate actively and hold government institutions accountable." On their account, the evidence is clear that "governance systems increase the prospects for peace when they are inclusive, participatory and accountable and have sufficient capacity to ensure security and provide the full range of public goods."[36]

There is, then, a series of political priorities that actors, both within countries and in the larger international community, can work toward to reduce war and build peace.

— The Vatican is correct when it associates democratic forms of government with peace, but there is an important complicating caveat. Established democracies are indeed less prone to war than countries with autocratic governments. Overall, they experience lower levels of internal political violence, such as terrorism, state repression, and mass atrocities. They have a very low risk of civil war, one that has for centuries been smaller than that of countries with dictatorial regimes. And when such conflicts do happen, they are significantly less deadly in democracies. Ethnic and territorial disputes within established democracies are far less likely to escalate to armed conflict, instead usually getting channeled into nonviolent political settlements, as long-standing cases such as Quebec and Scotland illustrate.[37]

Consolidated democracies also fight fewer wars against other countries. Especially notable here is what researchers call the phenomenon of "the democratic peace." This is the well-established fact that democracies almost never go to war with each other, something not true of other regime types. This means that while established democracies are somewhat more likely to avoid interstate wars overall, they are even more likely to establish lasting zones of nonviolent problem-solving among themselves, zones that can spread across the globe the more numerous democracies become.[38]

But note the qualifiers "established" and "consolidated" in the last two paragraphs. The peaceful effects of democracy are most pronounced for those countries that have built a set of stable, well-established, resilient democratic institutions. Countries that have just transitioned to democracy, on the other hand, can sometimes actually experience a higher risk of armed conflict, especially civil war. New political institutions often have a difficult time responding when recently liberated groups mobilize around long-suppressed grievances, when nationalist leaders emerge to compete for votes, or when members of the old regime, especially the military, act as violent spoilers. These risks are most acute in lower-income countries transitioning to democracy, or when the transition is the result of armed force overthrowing a former autocratic regime. Especially dangerous is when a country gets caught in a middle zone that political scientists call "anocracy," which is a politically unstable mix of some democratic and some autocratic elements.[39]

This does not mean rejecting the kind of prodemocracy work Catholic teaching endorses. Democracy's long-term benefits, including armed conflict reduction, are too important. Instead, it means that the Vatican is right to emphasize that work on behalf of democracy must be multidimensional and ongoing. Democracy does not automatically arrive when dictatorships end. It requires continuing efforts to build strong, effective, and truly democratic institutions.

— Consolidating a democratic form of government is obviously impossible if it never exists in the first place, so ongoing efforts to transform autocratic regimes into democratic ones is vital. This is difficult but certainly not impossible — in fact, it happens regularly around the world. As we saw in chapter 2, the least effective way to do this is through war, either internal armed rebellion or outside military interventions. These methods are less likely to bring down dictators and, when they do manage it, less likely to actually produce lasting democracy. A more effective approach is steady, multipoint pressure by activists, religious leaders, civic organizations, unions, independent journalists, and everyday citizens to open up more democratic space in such regimes, pushing them toward democratic reforms and transitions. Such efforts can also pave the way for more dramatic action in the form of mass nonviolent civil resistance campaigns that aim to bring down a dictatorial regime completely. As we also saw in chapter 2, such campaigns are more effective than armed force in defeating dictators and creating durable democracy. The international community can support these efforts by helping reform and resistance groups with training, technical assistance, and global attention to their cause, as well as by bringing their own pressure to bear on regimes through incentives, sanctions, and conditioning foreign aid on democratic reforms. While there are no guarantees of success, a mix of internal and external pressure can make a difference, successfully pushing nondemocratic regimes to gradually reform themselves out of existence or causing them to collapse in the face of mass noncooperation. Examples of success include South Africa, Serbia, Nepal, Greece, South Korea, Chile, the Philippines, and many more.[40]

Since the evidence on armed conflict is clear that it is not just democracy, but the depth and character of democracy that matters, work within countries, with external support where necessary, to build and sustain durable democratic institutions must be ongoing. This is especially important in new democracies, countries caught in that intermediate anocracy zone, and those at risk of backsliding into autocracy.

Democracies that most successfully avoid warfare are those that are inclusive. They facilitate broad-based participation and representation across a society rather than a winner-take-all ethos where leaders beholden to a bare majority rule for the sole benefit of their ethnic, religious, or regional group. This is why for new democracies, it is important not to rush into elections before building a stable institutional infrastructure for equitable democratic governance.[41] Since systematically excluding groups within a country from political representation, and thus from a fair distribution of government services, increases the risk of civil war, institutions that integrate multiple groups, disperse political power among them, and incentivize widespread participation by ordinary citizens are more effective in preventing armed conflict. As Peter Wallensteen points out, lowering the risk of civil war means giving "reasonable social and political space to all groups in the society." For example, parliamentary/prime minister systems that rely on proportional representation have a better track record of reducing armed conflict and creating enduring democracy than presidential systems that concentrate executive power in a single elected official. For some deeply divided societies, a formal power-sharing system—what political scientists call "consociationalism"—can reduce the risk of armed conflict, an approach, for instance, that was important to ending the Troubles in Northern Ireland. Another effective mechanism is devolving political power to geographic areas with a strong ethnic, religious, or regional identity, granting them significant autonomy over such things as tax, education, or language policies. These types of institutional arrangements integrate groups across a society by using mechanisms that encourage formal recognition, negotiation, and consensus building. They can effectively consolidate democracy and significantly lower the odds of political violence that escalates into warfare. As Cortright, Seyle, and Wall put it, "Research shows a strong connection between the degree of representation within a political system and the prospects for peace."[42]

Democratic systems that incorporate strong human rights protections, especially for ethnic, religious, or regional minorities, are more successful in creating inclusive political systems and reducing the risk of armed conflict. Meaningful guarantees of religious freedom, nondiscrimination in economic and social life, the right to vote and hold political office, freedom of assembly, protection against arbitrary arrest and imprisonment, language rights, and other civil liberties strengthen democracy and make peace more likely.[43]

The same is true of democratic systems where women are able to take part more fully in political life. Higher levels of female participation in government, especially legislative decision-making, are strongly correlated with lower levels of armed conflict. And there is an important feedback loop here too. Less discrimination against girls, especially in education, leads to higher socioeconomic status for women, which itself is associated with a greater likelihood that a country will be a democracy.[44]

Another important characteristic of strong and durable democracies with lower risks of armed conflict is a vibrant civil society. Nongovernmental but still public institutions — unions, professional and business associations, civic groups, religious bodies, and a diverse array of voluntary organizations — can build social trust, facilitate broad-based political participation by everyday citizens, and help hold government officials accountable. Civil society is especially important in lowering the risk of armed conflict within a country when it is able to provide "bridging forms of social capital" by connecting people across lines such as religion, ethnicity, or class.[45]

— Consolidated democracies prevent armed conflict, especially civil war, not only by being inclusive and broadly representative but also by effectively carrying out the essential functions of governing. Sufficient state capacity and good governance are critical to a democracy's success, including its ability to reduce the risk of warfare. This is an area where internal actors, and their external supporters in the international community, can also make a difference, especially during transitions to democracy. Cortright, Seyle, and Wall argue that working for effective and responsive governance "may be the most effective way to manage conflicts and prevent the outbreak of armed violence."[46]

Weak states without adequate governing capacity, particularly those just transitioning to democracy or those trapped in an unstable anocracy, often fall prey to political elites extracting national resources for their own profit. Unrestrained by the rule of law, such actions spill down to the local level through networks of systematic corruption and organized crime. This victimizes ordinary citizens, sabotages public services, erodes social trust, and undermines government legitimacy. As a result, such countries are more likely to experience civil war sparked by a mixture of public frustration, group grievance, and predatory armed groups. This leads the political scientist John Mueller to conclude that a great deal of warfare in the world today "is a function of the extent to which inadequate governments exist."[47]

Countering this means building capable and accountable governing institutions. These deliver public services—education, healthcare, unemployment benefits, dependable power, clean water, or basic government documents such as birth certificates, business licenses, identification cards, and property titles—in reliable and nonbiased ways. Especially important is the rule of law. Countries with an independent and responsive legal system that delivers public safety and fair access to the courts, where police protect rather than abuse ordinary citizens, and where due process rights are upheld enjoy a lower risk of civil war. Initiatives that provide information to local citizens about government performance—such as police responses to reported crimes, teacher absentee rates, or what percentage of education funding actually reaches local schools—can increase political participation that holds officials accountable and improves services. Giugale points out that government legitimacy requires building public trust, and "the only way to create trust is through results." Notably, there is a military-governance connection here too: the more the armed forces are under civilian government control, and the lower the country's overall military budget and levels of foreign military aid, the more robust and reliable public services to civilians become, and the less likely the country is to experience armed conflict.[48]

One of the biggest threats to good governance is corruption. Like chronic injuries that undermine athletic performance, corruption continually weakens the effectiveness and responsiveness of governing institutions. Wallensteen calls it "the single most effective way in which a democracy can lose its legitimacy." And high levels of corruption are associated with a greater risk for violence and civil war.[49]

Fighting corruption is not easy, but it is possible. Among measures that can help are a more professionalized civil service, random municipal audits with publicized results, a free and independent press, incentives and protections for whistleblowers, an independent judiciary, and more consistent prosecution of companies, government officials, and individuals for corruption. Greater transparency also has a positive impact. This can include publishing local and national budgets online and having nongovernmental organizations that produce and publicize corruption rankings within and among countries. Publicly tracking and verifying the flow of revenues and payments from oil, gas, and mining operations can be especially helpful. So too is diverting more profits from such operations directly to citizens as dividends rather than through government officials. As these measures indicate, a multifaceted approach that includes top-down anticorruption actions by government institutions, but also consistent grassroots pressure from civil society groups, is most promising.[50]

— Let's end this section on political factors that promote peace where we started it: with their connection to economic and social factors. Effective, responsive, and accountable governance, especially where the rule of law is strong and corruption is low, creates a positive feedback loop with the kinds of economic development that also promote peace.

In their book *The Locust Effect*, Gary Haugen and Victor Boutros show how one of the biggest obstacles to economic growth and poverty reduction in the developing world is poor governance, especially the routine insecurity and "predatory violence" that average people face in the absence of the rule of law. During colonialism, police and judicial systems were designed not to protect local people, but rather to facilitate their exploitation. When developing countries gained their independence from colonial powers, in many cases new political and economic elites simply kept such systems in place for their own use. The result in such countries is that everyday citizens have little protection from street violence, organized crime rackets, and police shakedowns.

They cannot rely on the judicial system to establish titles to property, enforce contracts, or resolve disputes. For Haugen and Boutros, countries are unlikely to make progress in reducing poverty or boosting economic growth without fixing this fundamental failure of governance and the rule of law.[51]

In another example, Giugale points out that developing countries collect only about half the tax revenue, as a percentage of GDP, that wealthier countries collect. Stronger state capacity would help them capture more revenue from economic development, especially from multinational firms extracting resources such as minerals and fossil fuels, which could then be invested in a more diversified economy, infrastructure improvements, poverty reduction, education, healthcare, and other measures that reduce the likelihood of armed conflict.[52]

Overall, countries provide a strong foundation for economic development when they have capable and representative institutions, predictable rules upheld by law, property rights balanced by effective economic regulations, and robust social welfare provisions. Such development, in turn, is associated with reduced corruption, greater governing capacity, better delivery of public services, and improved health and education outcomes. So it is the combination of inclusive and accountable democratic institutions, effective governance, and economic and social development that improves the odds of peace, confirming the "integral" or "authentic" development approach articulated by Catholic teaching.[53]

AREAS OF PERSISTENT ARMED CONFLICT

Recall from chapter 3 the importance of focusing on regions where countries experience chronic stop-and-start warfare. Breaking these cycles of persistent, recurring war has the potential to dramatically reduce global armed conflict, and it is the most effective way to prevent mass atrocities such as ethnic cleansing and genocide.

This process starts with the international community's using its capacity for global governance to push for and facilitate cease-fires, negotiated settlements, and peacekeeping operations. But it is crucial to follow up this initial stage with longer-term efforts to build peace. Such efforts address the factors we just saw at work in this current chapter. In postconflict societies, the international community can support local actors in their work for economic, social, and political conditions that make lasting peace more likely.

Rapid economic growth after a conflict reduces the odds of its recurring, and well-timed foreign aid can help boost such growth. Similarly, reducing military spending after a conflict, shifting government priorities instead to human welfare services such as education or healthcare, reduces the likelihood of a conflict's restarting.[54]

Political factors are even more important. Lasting peace in postconflict societies requires reestablishing state capacity and the rule of law, providing reliable government services to the population, including basic physical security.[55] It is important to establish this first, before broader political reforms and democratic elections. This sets the stage for more successful transitions to democracy after armed conflicts, transitions that do reduce the odds of war breaking out again, especially in proportional and consociational power-sharing systems, which coopt and incorporate former rivals. Factors such as strong minority rights and a robust civil society have similarly positive impacts. When, following an armed conflict, a democratic regime is replacing a formerly oppressive dictatorial one, a combination of trials, amnesties, and truth and reconciliation commissions addressing those complicit in the former regime's abuses reduces the odds of war recurring. And the greater the social and political incorporation of women, the less likely the return of war becomes. In their work, researchers Jacqueline Demeritt, Angela Nichols, and Eliza Kelly find that "with no women in the legislature, the risk of relapse clearly increases over time. When 35 percent of the legislature is female, this relationship virtually disappears, and the risk of relapse is near zero."[56]

— Whether it is in such postconflict societies specifically, or in countries around the world more generally, Catholic teaching is right to emphasize the long game on behalf of peace. Patient, ongoing work on behalf of more just societies — those with low poverty, widely shared prosperity, equitable access to basic human welfare services, gender equity, minority rights, a robust civil society, inclusive and accountable democratic institutions, and effective governance — can dramatically reduce the frequency of war. Catholic teaching is therefore correct in its shorthand formula: If you want peace, work for justice.

CHAPTER 5

ABOLISHING WAR

This book opened with the papal mantra "Never again war!"[1] Catholic teaching really is committed to reaching that "never again" part. It is explicitly abolitionist, demanding that the world eliminate war entirely.

The Second Vatican Council writes in *Gaudium et Spes*, "Divine Providence urgently demands of us that we free ourselves from the age-old slavery of war." John Paul II states, "War should belong to the tragic past, to history, it should find no place on humanity's agenda for the future," and so we should "proceed resolutely toward outlawing war completely." And Francis says it is finally "time to stop!" and "give up the way of arms." He pleads, "May humanity understand that the moment has come to abolish war, to erase it from human history."[2]

In *Centesimus Annus*, John Paul II writes, "Just as the time has finally come when in individual States a system of private vendetta and reprisal has given way to the rule of law, so too a similar step forward is now urgently needed in the international community." This echoes Paul VI, who in urging the world to abolish war, states, "You cannot eliminate unless you replace with something else." That something else is precisely the methods of greater global governance and justice promotion that we examined in the last two chapters. For the church, the comprehensive tools that it advocates for preventing armed conflict have the potential to reduce war to zero, leaving the world with plenty of problems, including other forms of violence, but better off for being finally free of war.[3]

— How can the church think such an ambitious goal as abolishing all war is possible? The answer lies in its teaching on structural sin and the possibility of progress without perfection. For Catholic teaching, sin is expressed in the actions of individual persons, but through such actions it can also become embedded in "social situations and institutions" and in "unjust systems and structures." These can take many forms, from political oppression to systematic poverty to environmental destruction, and war is clearly among them; Francis, for example, states that "sin is manifest in all its destructive power in wars." According to the Second Vatican Council, a key dimension of these "structures of sin" is how they shape the thinking and behavior of persons through the power exercised by "the social circumstances in which they live and are immersed from their birth." John Paul II echoes this in his own statements on the subject. Because structural sin can fundamentally shape how individuals are "conditioned, incited and influenced," it explains how individual sinfulness can "grow stronger, spread, and become the source of other sins, and so influence people's behavior."[4]

Since people are "conditioned" by the structural sin surrounding them, it shapes the way they perceive reality. It makes its institutionalized injustice appear to be just-the-way-things-are, seeming to foreclose any possibility of change. John Paul II labels this "supposed impossibility of changing the world" an especially pernicious aspect of structural sin. But it is one he urges humanity to resist. While sin itself will always be part of this world, its specific manifestations in particular social structures are never locked in. These can be changed, even abolished. We can find "the path to be followed in order to overcome" them. In *Centesimus Annus*, he states that "to destroy such structures and replace them with more authentic forms of living in community" is possible, though "a task that demands courage and patience."[5] This is why Francis, in calling for war's abolition, says: "War should not be something that is inevitable. We should not accustom ourselves to war."[6]

Catholic teaching offers a nuanced understanding of social progress. The church does not believe that full, complete, perfect justice and peace are possible in the world as it is; that must await God's kingdom. The Second Vatican Council states that to some extent imperfections caused by sin will always "contaminate" the "social sphere," and John Paul II writes that "man, who was created for freedom, bears within himself the wound of original sin, which constantly draws him toward evil and puts him in need of redemption."[7]

But, while a perfect world is not possible, we have seen in the last several chapters that a more just, peaceful, and humane one certainly is. Why else would the church spend so much time advocating for work on behalf of such a world? John Paul II states that perfection's being out of reach this side of God's kingdom "can never be an excuse for lack of concern for people in their concrete personal situations and in their social, national and international life." It really is possible to, in the words of Vatican II, "build a better world," one less violent, more just, and "genuinely human." Indeed, the council argues that the perfection promised in the coming kingdom should actually inspire work for greater justice and peace in this world, something echoed by Benedict XVI in *Caritas in Veritate* when he writes that efforts to "shape the earthly city in unity and peace" are "an anticipation and a prefiguration of the undivided city of God."[8]

The focus here is not trying to change human nature but rather changing variable human institutions. The Second Vatican Council speaks in terms of "improvement of customs and institutions," and Benedict XVI of altering "structures, institutions, culture." For John XXIII, "If there is to be any improvement in human institutions, the work must be done slowly and deliberately." Such work can reform, transform, and even abolish particular institutionalized practices, even if human nature itself remains the same.[9]

This approach is why Catholic teaching does not consider the goal of a better world, including one free of war, unrealistic. John Paul II says of such efforts, "Nothing will be lost or will have been in vain." Francis declares, "It will not trouble us to be deemed naïve for choosing peace." And Benedict XVI writes, "Peace is not a dream or something utopian; it is possible." Indeed, Paul VI argues that those who think progress is not possible are the ones "not realistic enough" about how the world actually works.[10]

A sense of hope, rooted in guarded optimism about the reality of human progress, is one of the most consistent themes in Catholic teaching over the last century. It continually points to how things really can get better, even if the path to improvement includes challenges and setbacks. According to John Paul II, the church has "an optimistic vision of history and work, that is to say of the perennial value of authentic human achievements."[11] Vatican documents regularly invoke "progress," positive "evolution," the "road to more thorough development," and humanity's "advance toward maturity." They celebrate "the positive signs at work in humanity's present situation" and the "keener sense of human dignity" driving advancements on behalf of human rights, democracy and the rule of law, poverty reduction, disease eradication, educational access, and, notably, declines in armed conflict as well.[12]

— This, then, is the diagnosis Catholic teaching offers. Human beings in this world will always be imperfect, marked by sin. Greed, deceit, violence, and other vices will always be with us. But that doesn't mean everything always remains the same. Particular social, political, and economic circumstances are not constant. Just as they sometimes get worse, they can also get better, sometimes much better. With work, there can be real improvements in specific areas of human life. Since we construct social institutions over time, we can also deconstruct them and replace them with new, better, more humane ones.

Recall from the top of this chapter John Paul II's highlighting, as inspiration for ending war at the international level, how countries gradually replaced bloody vendetta systems with more effective legal institutions. He is not suggesting that eliminating vendetta systems made countries perfectly just, only that they are better off without this particular violent practice. Francis makes a similar point when celebrating the formal abolition of chattel slavery, even as he condemns continuing forms of human trafficking and labor exploitation. Abolishing chattel slavery did not produce a world free of injustice, and it even ushered in some new forms of injustice "akin to slavery," but it was nonetheless an important achievement for humanity.[13] For the Vatican, it is possible to eliminate some forms of institutionalized violence without having to eliminate all violence or change human nature or create a perfectly just world.

The best example of this in Catholic teaching is the death penalty. For much of its history the church accepted capital punishment as a necessary practice to punish lawbreaking and protect the common good in a violent and sinful world. Augustine justified it in terms remarkably similar to those he used in justifying war (and slavery, for that matter). Over the last century, however, as Catholic teaching grew increasingly critical of the death penalty, it emerged as a leading advocate for the worldwide abolition of the practice in favor of alternatives. Calling for capital punishment's elimination does not mean Catholic teaching has changed its fundamental understanding of sin or of the human person. It is under no illusions that ending the death penalty will produce perfectly just societies, or even criminal justice systems free of other injustices, which is why the church continues to call for reform in areas such as solitary confinement. Its position is more modest, though still important. Eliminating this particular unjust and violent institution is possible. Doing so will leave plenty of other injustices and forms of violence, but that does not negate the real moral progress produced by its abolition. All else being equal, a world without capital punishment is better than one with it.[14] The Vatican claims the same is true of war.

WAR AS AN INVENTION

Almost all human beings, across the entire history of our species, have had the natural cognitive and physical capacity to speak Japanese, ride a bike, or play chess. But nobody spontaneously speaks Japanese. Or rides a bike. And games of chess don't just randomly break out. Japanese, bikes, and chess all have to exist first. Likewise, it is entirely possible that the greatest natural basketball player or opera singer or competitive hot dog eater ever born never had the chance to do any of these things for the simple reason that they hadn't been invented yet.

In her famous essay "War Is Only an Invention — Not a Biological Necessity," Margaret Mead argues that while warfare is common among humans, it is not universal, and our species didn't always engage in it. Instead, humans invented it, just as we invented "writing, marriage, cooking our food instead of eating it raw, trial by jury or burial of the dead." Not all societies across human history, including ones with high levels of interpersonal violence, have fought wars. This was often because the very "idea of warfare" was missing, and "this idea is as essential to really carrying on war as an alphabet or a syllabary is to writing."[15] Under this understanding of wars, a society won't fight them if it doesn't actually have the institution, just as it won't fight duels, burn witches, play football, or post TikTok videos if doesn't have these institutions either.

For Mead, the fact that war is an invention doesn't mean that it is not now deeply rooted in human affairs: "Once an invention is known and accepted, men do not easily relinquish it." But war's being an invention does mean that it is not inherently part of the human condition, an inescapable part of our nature. As with other long-standing inventions, humanity can eventually set it aside if its harms become recognized widely enough and better alternatives emerge to replace it.[16] Not all of the ways our species does things last forever.

While there are ongoing debates over the origins of warfare, there is much to support Mead's view. Summarizing the evidence, the anthropologist Douglas Fry writes that "humans are not warlike by nature," and "war is not ancient."[17] Fighting wars is not a universal trait among humans: there are plenty of nonwarring societies in the historical and anthropological record; it is common for communities within larger societies, such as the Jains or the Amish, to reject all war; and many modern countries have successfully opted out of the war system. While capacities for both violent aggression and nonviolent conflict resolution go back to the origins of our species, war as such did not exist for well over 90 percent of our long existence on earth. It is only in the last ten to fourteen thousand years that large-scale, impersonal (rather than targeting specific individuals in a feud), and organized armed conflict emerged.[18] Indeed, as the military historian John Keegan points out, most of human history exists "below the military horizon" — that is, before the rise of social structures and political authority capable of fielding, directing, and equipping armies. On his account, war actually required *suppressing* human nature, since it meant imposing the kind of discipline that overrides fight-or-flight impulses, forcing soldiers to march in an orderly fashion toward an enemy intending to kill them and to hold their attack until instructed by their commanders.[19]

So if Mead is right that warfare is not a universal human trait — that it is an invention rather than an inherent part of our nature — is she also right that this means we are not stuck with it forever? Can we discard it as something humans no longer do? Her essay raises, but does not pursue in much depth, resemblances to other violent inventions in human history that we have either entirely or mostly done away with. Let's consider some of these to see if they suggest whether something similar can happen for war.

POTENTIAL PARALLELS

Is it possible to actually eliminate deeply rooted forms of institutionalized violence such as war? History suggest the answer is yes, but it can be a difficult and uneven process, and one that can still leave plenty of injustices in its wake.

As we saw earlier in this chapter, capital punishment was once so common a punishment for lawbreaking as to be unremarkable. For millennia, and all around the world, people were routinely put to death for things that today most consider minor crimes or no crimes at all: pickpocketing, adultery, poaching, forgery, blasphemy, or sodomy. That this was the only way to deter crime and protect public order was just common sense. In the words of a nineteenth-century American magazine article, "Murder never has been, and never can be checked, by a slighter penalty than death!" In 1843, a Pennsylvania General Assembly committee declared it "clearly the law of nature." As James Megivern demonstrates in his survey of the institution's history, capital punishment was justified through explicit parallels to war; both were deemed a necessary form of violence to protect the community, and doing without them would be impossible.[20]

This is why early proponents of capital punishment's abolition were dismissed as sentimental and unrealistic about the realities of evil in the world. In the United States, death penalty defenders called these early abolitionists "dreamers in a world of living men," naïve optimists marked by "soft sentimentality," and "mostly females of very tender feelings, and men of a similar spirit." Capital punishment's critics obviously "never had a brother, a wife, or a child murdered by the cruel hands of any ruffian," and listening to them would bring "every kind of evil" and lead to "social ruin."[21]

Yet, today, as the political scientist Sangmin Bae details, even though the death penalty "has a history as old as society itself, and was not considered a human rights violation until the last decades of the twentieth century," the majority of countries around the world have now banned it, most others who retain it in their laws don't actually carry it out, and in the very small number of countries that still use it, including the United States, it is remarkably rare by historical standards.[22]

Legal history furnishes another powerful example. It was once common in many societies around the world, stretching all the way back to the Code of Hammurabi, to resolve disputes and determine guilt or innocence in criminal matters through trial by ordeal or combat. In medieval Europe, for instance, authorities addressed matters such as theft, murder, fraud, land ownership, paternity, adultery, and heresy through rituals that let God signal the just outcome. This meant people routinely fought to the death using a variety of weapons, most often a simple club and shield; or they would endure being burned by boiling water or molten metal to see how their wounds healed; or they would be thrown into lakes and rivers to see if they sank or floated. A Norwegian law, for example, specified that "if a man is charged with having carnal dealings with cattle of any sort," the bailiff will require him "carry the hot iron" to determine his guilt or innocence. And a German law required that if a woman was suspected of killing her husband, her nearest relative had to "prove her innocence in battle, or, if she has not a champion, let her be sent to trial by the nine red-hot ploughshares." These practices lasted for centuries, longer in fact than today's institution of trial by jury has been around.[23]

As with the death penalty, trials by ordeal and combat were widely understood to be crucial for social order. They protected the innocent, prevented crime, and compelled people to keep their oaths. As one medieval European observer said, "It is better that they fight in the field with clubs than that they commit perjury." Even if some particular outcomes seemed unjust, to deny their legitimacy was to attack religion itself. As the historian Robert Bartlett puts it, "For the most part, people found ways of retaining a belief in the value of the ordeal as an institution even when they doubted its verdict in a given case."[24] People understood that these rituals, while often brutal, were necessary and came with divine sanction.

Yet, today, the thought of resolving disputes and determining guilt or innocence by having people come before judges to club each other to death or plunge their hands into boiling water or walk across red-hot strips of metal seems absurd.

Dueling was also once widespread and deadly serious. Andrew Jackson may have killed up to eighteen people in duels. Alexander Hamilton famously fell on the same ground and with the same pistols that claimed his son's life. The composer George Frideric Handel fought a duel over being denied his turn on a harpsicord, the astronomer Tycho Brahe had his nose cut off during one sparked by someone's questioning his mathematical prowess, and the son of Francis Scott Key, author of the national anthem, was killed by a friend after they disagreed about how fast a steamboat was traveling.[25]

As Mead points out, duels can't just break out; they only exist in societies where the institution, with all its social expectations and detailed rules, exists and has legitimacy. For instance, in Europe and the United States, where the duel existed for centuries, written manuals detailing procedures for initiating and fighting them were widely read, and young men enrolled in training courses to learn how to use dueling's specialized weapons. Refusing a duel would mean family disgrace, social ostracism, and likely the loss of one's job. It depended for its power on what the historian V. G. Kiernan terms "an extreme form of social compulsion." This is why the historical record is full of people who went to their deaths reluctantly. A British colonel, for instance, wrote this the night before he died in a duel: "I commit my soul to Almighty God, in hopes of his mercy and pardon for the irreligious step I now (in compliance with the unwarrantable customs of this wicked world) put myself under the necessity of taking."[26]

Like war, the duel was widely accepted as necessary in a world where only the threat of force could restrain abusive behavior. Its proponents produced comparative studies they claimed showed societies with dueling were more peaceful than those without it, since, in order to avoid being challenged to duels, people avoided aggression and took care to be more honest, civil, and respectful toward others.[27] This is why the duel enjoyed wide popular legitimacy and its early critics were dismissed as unrealistic, sentimental, and spineless. John Lyde Wilson, a governor of South Carolina in the 1830s, argued that dueling was based on "the first law of nature, self-preservation," and that just as "an oppressed nation has the right to appeal to arms in defense of its liberty and the happiness of its people, there can be no argument used in support of such appeal which will not apply with equal force to individuals" who engage in duels. Under Napoleon, the French government rejected an antidueling proposal by pointing to times where "it is impossible for a man to right himself otherwise than by a duel." And one nineteenth-century supporter of dueling declared that those "who have opposed dueling are either fools or cowards," since dueling is necessary to protect each individual as "a strong and independent power."[28]

Yet, today, the thought of a couple of acquaintances or co-workers exchanging notes over some slight, meeting at dawn, choosing weapons, and calmly setting about to kill each other seems a ridiculous anachronism.

— While the how-could-they-have-done-that nature of dueling and trials by ordeal and combat is now almost comical, the scope and brutality of chattel slavery across human history remains morally difficult to fathom. Arising around the same time as war, slavery has been closely intertwined with it. Many armies over the millennia used enslaved soldiers, and many other people were, in turn, captured and enslaved during wars. Like war, slavery spread to become a global institution. According to the historian Orlando Patterson, it "has existed in some form in every region of the world, at all levels of sociopolitical development, and among all major ethnic groups." As with war, the institution is inseparable from its pervasive and intense violence; in addition to being regularly worked to death, enslaved persons were subject to routine beatings, rape, mutilation, and summary execution. And slavery's systematic dehumanization was, if anything, more complete than war's. In Patterson's influential *Slavery and Social Death*, he details how thoroughly chattel slavery stripped people of their dignity and any independent social existence, turning them into disposable human tools. When he was an enslaved child, the American George Washington Albright remembered his father's sale, saying owners "thought no more of selling a man away from his wife, or a mother away from her children, than of sending a cow or a horse out of state." As the word "chattel" in "chattel slavery" indicates, the institution treated persons as equivalent to livestock.[29]

There was no such thing as spontaneous chattel slavery. Slave societies depended on a comprehensive social and economic infrastructure woven into daily life, one governed by detailed laws and regulations. These were supported by a powerful belief in the institution's legitimacy. Aristotle argued that since certain people lacked reason, they were "by their nature slaves," and the "use made of slaves, too, departs but little from that made of other animals." Augustine considered slavery something supported by the "judgement of God" and "appointed by that law which enjoins the preservation of the natural order and forbids its disturbance." It was considered part of the human condition, something necessary for social stability. A South Carolina court decision upholding the institution declared, "Servitude has existed under various forms, from the deluge to the present time." And the American writer George Fitzhugh took the "naturalness and necessity of slavery" for granted, calling it an "indispensable" institution necessary for "good order."[30]

As societies that go to war have regarded war as necessary, so slave societies considered slavery necessary to protect their way of life. It was, if often unpleasant, indispensable to national wealth, power, and security. The doctor and scientist Edward Bancroft argued that many things "repugnant to humanity, may be excused, on account of their necessity for self-preservation." An eighteenth-century British defender, Malachy Postlethwayt, stated: "The Negroe-Trade and the natural Consequences resulting from it, may be justly esteemed an inexhaustible Fund of Wealth and Naval Power to this Nation." And the American William Henry Holcombe considered slavery necessary for "industrial prosperity and the peace of nations."[31]

One of the remarkable things about chattel slavery is that although across its long history there was plenty of resistance by its victims—revolts, escapes, attempts to carve out small spaces for dignity—and there were occasional exhortations to treat those in bondage less brutally, it was not until the late eighteenth century that a sustained movement to eliminate the very institution itself emerged. Not surprisingly, given how entrenched chattel slavery was, these early abolitionists faced withering criticism. They were accused of being sentimental and unrealistic, naïve about how the world really worked. Their critics routinely raised the specter of violence unleashed by freed slaves on defenseless whites, especially the rape of white women, calling abolition a "proposal for the butchery of women and children, for scenes of lust and rapine, and of arson and murder." In England, the Earl of Abingdon said, "The Order, and Subordination, and Happiness of the whole habitable Globe is threatened" by abolitionism. US vice president John C. Calhoun considered it a "suicidal policy," and in Brazil, proslavery lawmakers called it "a crime, robbery, theft, and a communist plot."[32]

Yet, today, chattel slavery serves for most people as a go-to example of a moral evil long practiced but now rejected.

— So how did humanity discard—either completely or almost completely—these once-ubiquitous instances of institutional violence? While there was no uniform blueprint, the process usually saw a long, patient effort by abolitionists to condemn them and press for action to gradually dismantle and replace them. This meant creating a cycle where cultural attitudes shifted against such institutions, effectively delegitimizing them, which helped move government policy from supporting to suppressing them, something that in turn eroded their social acceptance even more. The result saw new cultural norms and expectations arise, ones that eventually led people to consider such institutions unjust and anachronistic. Often, this unfolded as societies developed newer, alternative institutions to replace those they were abandoning.

It is important to realize that this process was usually gradual and uneven. It moved in stops and starts, often facing setbacks on the way to abolition. It could also leave behind long-lasting remnants of the old institution. Even more significantly, the institution's replacements could themselves embody their own injustices. Abolition sometimes left new forms of institutionalized violence in its wake, a pattern consistent with Catholic teaching's emphasis on the possibility of human progress but not human perfection.

For the death penalty, an international movement to abolish it emerged in the nineteenth century, and several generations of activists emphasized its cruel and arbitrary nature, seeking to portray it as barbaric and unworthy of modern civilizations. By the mid-to-late twentieth century, this became a powerful international norm, often embodied in global and regional treaties, which spread rapidly around the world. As Bae details, even where a country's citizens may have supported its use, political leaders moved to abolish it in order to bolster their country's international reputation. The growing global norm made still having capital punishment an embarrassment, and leaders did not want their country to appear archaic in comparison to others. But, of course, just because countries eliminated or dramatically curtailed the death penalty doesn't mean they freed themselves from many other injustices embedded in their criminal justice systems.[33]

Seven centuries earlier in medieval Europe, ordinary people became more and more willing to express doubts about the accuracy of trials by ordeal and combat. Knowing the people involved and then seeing the outcomes, was justice really done? Charges of their being arbitrary or even rigged became more common. Taking up these criticisms, the clergy, who had key roles in overseeing these institutions, began to turn against them. Church officials wanting to centralize religious authority in Rome increasingly considered trials by ordeal and combat disorderly and unpredictable spectacles, irrational expressions of provincial superstition. They began developing theological critiques of the hubris involved in trying to force God's hand through such displays. The growing practice of regular lay confession also gave clergy a new and powerful alternative social role as a replacement. At the same time, secular leaders began turning to new methods of legal enforcement. The decline and eventual disappearance of trials by ordeal and combat track closely to the rise of inquisitorial methods that often relied on judicial torture to secure confessions—a new form of ordeal—and trial by jury—a new form of legal combat between two opposing parties.[34]

Dueling saw a similar collapse of legitimacy. Antidueling societies regularly repudiated the practice as lawless and self-indulgent. Popular understandings of honor shifted from endorsing violence to endorsing dignity and restraint. And the press began to denounce rather than celebrate duelists. Where the public once admired a man willing to duel, it eventually saw him as ridiculous and deserving of mockery. One nineteenth-century observer remarked that "ridicule at last did more than morality to kill dueling." Where once refusing a challenge could cost a man his reputation, his family honor, and his job, now accepting one could endanger all three. And legal incentives shifted as well. As public attitudes changed, governments began effectively enforcing antidueling laws. Where killing someone in a duel once enjoyed legal impunity, it could now bring a murder charge. Finally, the rise of alternatives also played a role in dueling's eclipse. In the nineteenth century, codes of ethics within professions, more formal workplace rules, and laws against libel and slander emerged to provide alternative ways to punish rude behavior and attacks on a person's reputation. Around the same time, a host of amateur sports—boxing, rugby, football, basketball, and others—arose with standard rules and governing bodies. These spread in popularity and provided young men in particular with a set of alternative, less lethal ways to prove their strength and courage against each other.[35]

Given chattel slavery's brutality, global scope, and deep connection to the wealth and power of nations, its abolition may be the most telling parallel to war. In the late eighteenth century, it seemed unassailable. It had been around for as long as recorded human history, it had become deeply woven into the social and legal fabric of societies around the world, and it had grown into a globally integrated economic system with broad legitimacy and powerful political support. But only a century later, in 1888, Brazil became the last major country to abolish it. In the words of David Brion Davis, the Pulitzer Prize–winning historian of chattel slavery, its abolition was "one of the most extraordinary events in history," one made possible by a "profound transformation in moral perception" that opened people's eyes to "the full horror of a social evil to which mankind had been blind for centuries" and ultimately "removed slavery from the list of supposedly inevitable misfortunes of life."[36]

At the height of its power, chattel slavery's foundations began to crack. Enslaved people increasingly organized to resist it, both through armed rebellions and, more frequently but often less noticeably, through nonviolent resistance techniques such as strikes and other forms of noncooperation. Critics tirelessly condemned it as a barbaric violation of basic human equality and dignity, producing a stream of lectures, essays, and novels highlighting its injustice and sheer brutality. The most powerful of these were testimonials and memoirs by those who had themselves escaped slavery. As with dueling, the balance of popular opinion in societies with slavery gradually shifted from considering the institution necessary to protect a lawful social order to considering it a violent, anachronistic threat to such an order.[37]

As with other forms of institutional violence, shifting public attitudes forced changes in government action. Here chattel slavery was especially vulnerable, since it was impossible without a vast infrastructure of government laws and policies. Once political leaders began to dismantle these, the institution could not survive. In some countries, such as the United States, this happened suddenly and violently, but most countries saw a more gradual process that phased out chattel slavery by, for instance, banning the slave trade, extending protection to those who escaped slavery, automatically emancipating people once they turned a certain age, legally sunsetting the institution, and compensating former owners of enslaved persons once it ended.[38]

However, these domestic actions did not happen in a vacuum. They were often the result of sustained international pressure. Abolishing chattel slavery was one of the first instances of what is known as a "global prohibition regime," which is a coordinated international campaign by states, intergovernmental organizations, and nongovernmental groups to control or eliminate a particular practice, usually through global treaties backed by monitoring and enforcement mechanisms. (Other examples have included piracy on the high seas, counterfeiting, poaching endangered species, and biological weapons.) As abolitionists began successfully ending chattel slavery in their own countries, they turned to organizing an international effort to press other countries to do the same, one that could lend support to domestic resistance within those countries. Moral appeals were certainly important, but creating and enforcing an international norm against chattel slavery also required a mixture of sanctions and incentives that convinced a country's leaders that they were better off renouncing it. This eventually created a tipping point that isolated the few countries still permitting the institution, which only added to the pressure that they not be the last ones clinging to a practice now seen by much of the world as backward and barbaric. Once this tipping point was reached, chattel slavery's final collapse as a global institution happened fairly rapidly.[39]

Abolishing chattel slavery obviously did not end every kind of coercive toil. Human trafficking, child labor, forced sex work, desperation-level wages, cast systems, and other abuses exist around the world today. And after abolition, formerly enslaved people often found themselves under new forms of debt bondage and forced apprenticeship systems. In most countries, they and their descendants experienced ongoing segregation, discrimination, and socially sanctioned violence. In the United States, for instance, publicly lynching Black citizens—complete with special trains to bring in spectators, children released from school early, and ice cream vendors—flourished in the post-Reconstruction period, especially in the Jim Crow South. And most of

Europe's brutal colonization of the African continent happened after chattel slavery's abolition.[40]

So, if abolishing chattel slavery didn't eliminate all forms of forced labor, and even saw new types of economic exploitation and institutionalized violence emerge, was it worth it? The answer is clearly yes. Given the historical length, depth, and breadth of the institution's cruel assault on human dignity, and the enormous suffering endured by its countless human victims, its abolition still amounts to a remarkable instance of moral progress. On balance, a world without chattel slavery is better than one with it. Those forms of exploitation and violence that remained or emerged after its fall should not negate the fall's importance. Rather, they point to how critical Catholic teaching's call for continuing work on behalf of a more just and peaceful world remains. In the Vatican's formulation, perfection remains out of reach, but genuine progress is both possible and an ongoing imperative.

ABOLISHING WAR IS POSSIBLE

The historical record demonstrates that humanity can indeed set aside widespread and deeply ingrained forms of institutionalized violence, ones formerly considered an inescapable part of the human condition. This suggests that abolishing war, as the Catholic Church urges, is at least possible. Why, then, is this possibility met with such widespread skepticism? Why do most people have such a difficult time imagining a world without war?

One answer is the way socially embedded forms of institutionalized violence shape thinking. Recall from the top of this chapter how Catholic teaching says structural sin "conditions" the way people perceive reality, making its manifestations seem inevitable, as just the way the world works, and therefore impossible to change, a view John Paul II pushed so hard against. The anthropologist Mary Douglas echoes this in her work detailing how a social institution can powerfully influence thinking, shaping the way people within it understand the world. It forms a "system of knowledge" that creates a "self-validating truth," one that people reinforce by "squeezing each other's ideas into common shape." The institution is accepted as self-evidently the way humans "naturally behave," thus basing "its rightness in reason and in nature." This is why "rules that now seem to us moderns monstrously unjust did not strike our forebears as wrong."[41] As we saw from the examples of institutionalized violence above, it is only when such institutions weaken or collapse entirely that most people recognize that things didn't have to be that way. It is entirely possible that the same may eventually be true of war.

Another reason people struggle to imagine a world free of war is that they assume this means more than it actually does, that it requires a world free of injustice, political violence, power, and countries pursuing their national interests. But all these things can still exist without war, just as unjust policing, wrongful convictions, harsh prison conditions, deadly fights sparked by insults, coerced labor, economic exploitation, and racial discrimination can all still exist in a world without capital punishment, trials by ordeal and combat, dueling, or chattel slavery. A world in which humanity manages to abolish war will likely look much like it does today, since war is actually a pretty rare occurrence for the average country and its citizens, and it would leave plenty of other forms of violence (mass shootings in the United States, drug cartel violence in Mexico, religious rioting in India, and so on) in need of being redressed too.

The thing about a deeply entrenched form of institutionalized violence is that it can remain dominant and largely unchallenged for centuries, but then unexpectedly experience a crisis of legitimacy, one that starts small and seems unrealistic, but then gradually grows stronger and, especially if viable alternatives and government opposition emerge, can set the institution on the path to abolition, seeing it diminish to the point that people eventually consider it an anachronism.

As the political scientist John Mueller points out in *The Remnants of War*, widespread condemnation of warfare as an institution in and of itself—as opposed to criticizing specific wars or calling for their more humane conduct—is only a little over a century old. While particular thinkers or smaller communities, usually religious, rejected war as such across its long history, the dominant view was that war was not only inevitable, but actually a positive good. Alexis de Tocqueville claimed it "enlarges the mind of a people and raises their character," G. W. F. Hegel that it prevents "social petrification and stagnation," and Igor Stravinsky that it "is necessary for human progress." It was not until the late nineteenth century that a significant portion of the wider global public begin to doubt war's necessity and legitimacy, and these doubts only accelerated in the twentieth century with its two devastating world wars. Indeed, the Catholic Church's comprehensive case against war, detailed in this book, is itself relatively recent, only taking shape over the last century! It too reflects and has helped drive this cultural turn against war.[42]

The spread of opposition to warfare itself in religious traditions, in broad-based peace movements, in global humanitarian organizations, and in literature and the arts has led some historians to suggest that this is a significant enough break with the past when it comes to attitudes toward war that it may amount to a crucial turning point for the institution. For instance, Keegan, in his *A History of Warfare*, notes that even for long-standing institutions, deep "cultural changes do occur," and "a profound change in civilisation's attitude toward war" seems to be happening. He argues that just as it once did with chattel slavery, humanity may have begun "distancing itself from the institution of warfare."[43]

It is possible, then, that humanity may already be on the road to war's abolition without realizing it, just as people in the later stages of dueling or ordeals or chattel slavery didn't know these institutions' days were numbered. If the process of abolition requires shifting social attitudes, the emergence of alternatives, and government policymakers willing to embrace these alternatives, then the abolition of war is certainly possible, since all of these ingredients already exist, even if each still needs to grow stronger.

PRESENT TRENDS AND ABOLITION'S PROSPECTS

The possibility that humanity can abolish war is encouraging. But possibility does not predict success; every day, things that are possible don't actually happen—winning a bet on basketball, beating cancer, healing a friendship, passing an exam. While eliminating war may be possible, for now it is still very much with us, and whether or not we will ultimately eliminate it is still an open question.

Among those who research armed conflict, there is considerable debate about the best ways to measure and track rates of warfare over time. Some argue that although there have been dips and spikes, the overall trend in warfare's frequency and death toll over the last several centuries is one of gradual decline, while others don't see evidence of long-term downward trends in the data.[44] As we saw in chapter 3, there does seem to have been a significant drop in interstate warfare—wars between two or more countries, as opposed to civil wars—since World War II, especially wars to secure colonies, capture territory, or redraw borders. The collapse of regular armed conflict between great powers, historically a particularly destructive form of warfare, is especially notable, something the political scientist Robert Jervis calls "a change of spectacular proportions, perhaps the single most striking discontinuity that the history of international politics has anywhere provided."[45]

The end of the Cold War did prompt a notable decline in overall armed conflict. Starting around 1990, the world saw drops in the frequency, duration, and deadliness of warfare. Around 2010, however, the number of wars began to increase again, though fortunately their overall magnitude—measured by factors such as fatalities, destructiveness, intensity, and length—did not rise back to late–Cold War levels, and while the rate of global war deaths per one hundred thousand people did rise, it remained low by historical standards. Notably, even as the number of armed conflicts began to rise after 2010, interstate war stayed at historic lows, with more civil wars, including those with foreign interventions, accounting for the increase.[46] Interstate war has clearly not disappeared though, as the 2022 Russian invasion of Ukraine illustrates.

Trends in armed conflict, then, offer reasons to hope for future declines toward abolition but also sobering reminders of war's stubborn persistence. What about recent trends in those broad economic, social, and political indicators of justice and human well-being that, as we saw in chapter 4, are connected to levels of warfare and that Catholic teaching emphasizes as crucial in helping create the long-term conditions for peace? Here too there are mixed signs.

In his book *Getting Better*, the economist Charles Kenny summarizes enormous worldwide progress over the last century in measures of health, nutrition, and education, characterizing it as a period of "rapid, historically unprecedented progress in quality of life." Since the late nineteenth century, infant mortality has declined by 75 percent and literacy has risen from 25 to 80 percent of the global population. Between 1900 and 2000, human life expectancy doubled. In the last several decades of the twentieth century alone, global infant mortality dropped by half, and literacy doubled in sub-Saharan Africa. From 1990 to 2010, extreme poverty around the world was cut in half. While much of this was driven by growth in large Asian countries such as China and India, average income in sub-Saharan Africa also rose by about a third in the first two decades of the twenty-first century. Indeed, according to Marcelo Giugale, 50 percent of Africa's population are expected to be middle class within a decade or so. The UN Human Development Index, which tracks indicators such as life expectancy, education levels, and per capita income, has, since its inception in 1990, shown steady global increases in every region of the world year after year (though 2020 and 2021 saw its life expectancy indicator level off and then dip slightly for the first time with the effects of the global COVID-19 pandemic). Of course, past progress does not negate the massive work that remains to address issues such as global poverty, public health, and access to education. And environmental damage, especially climate change, threatens such progress, especially in the poorest regions of the world.[47]

On the political side, in the post–World War II period, autocratic countries outnumbered democracies worldwide. The number of democracies gradually rose, however, and their growth dramatically accelerated with the end of the Cold War. Around 1990, they passed autocracies and anocracies to become the most common form of government. From the early 1970s to the mid-2000s, the number of democracies roughly doubled, rising to be around 60 percent of countries around the globe. But around 2010, democratic momentum stalled, the number of democracies worldwide started to decline slightly, and even more worrying, some countries that remained democracies saw erosions in democratic norms and the rule of law, putting them at greater risk of dropping back into anocracy or autocracy. There are still more democracies in the world than other types of regimes, but democracy has been in retreat over the last decade or so, something some scholars link to the rise in armed conflict during the same period.[48]

— So the evidence in this chapter suggests that Catholic teaching's call for humanity to abolish war, as other forms of institutional violence have been abolished before it, is certainly possible, but it is still not clear whether such abolition is probable. There are reasons for both hope and skepticism. Of course, while not ignoring the realities of a sinful world, the Catholic tradition asks humanity to embrace hope. In his final World Day of Peace message, John Paul II urged believers to "nourish an invincible hope which sustains their efforts to promote justice and peace," writing that in spite of "the personal and social sins which mark all human activity, hope constantly gives new impulse to the commitment to justice and peace, as well as firm confidence in the possibility of building a better world."[49] The future is what we make of it, and hope is part of what inspires continuing work for a more just and peaceful human community on this earth, one that can perhaps one day realize the frequent demand of John Paul II and his fellow popes: "Never Again War!"

RECOMMENDED READING

For readers who want to learn more, the books below are a great place to start. In selecting them, I tried to cover the full range of topics addressed in the book—the nature of war, its alternatives, how to prevent or even end it, Catholic teaching on war and peace. I also tried to include volumes from a variety of disciplines—social science, history, journalism, theology, ethics. Most importantly, I chose those that I think are especially influential, accessible, informative, and well written.

Ackerman, Peter, and Jack DuVall. 2000. *A Force More Powerful: A Century of Nonviolent Conflict*. New York: Palgrave.

Appiah, Kwame Anthony. 2010. *The Honor Code: How Moral Revolutions Happen*. New York: W.W. Norton.

Bacevich, Andrew J. 2005. *The New American Militarism: How Americans Are Seduced by War*. Oxford: Oxford University Press.

Berger, Rose Marie, Ken Butigan, Judy Coode, and Marie Dennis, eds. 2020. *Advancing Nonviolence and Just Peace in the Church and the World*. Brussels: Pax Christi International.

Bourke, Joanna. 1999. *An Intimate History of Killing: Face to Face Killing in 20th Century Warfare*. New York: Basic Books.

Cahill, Lisa Sowle. 1994. *Love Your Enemies: Discipleship, Pacifism, and Just War Theory*. Minneapolis: Fortress.

Chenoweth, Erica. 2021. *Civil Resistance: What Everyone Needs to Know*. Oxford: Oxford University Press.

Chenoweth, Erica, and Maria J. Stephan. 2011. *Why Civil Resistance Works: The Strategic Logic of Nonviolent Conflict*. New York: Columbia University Press.

Cortright, David, Conor Seyle, and Kristen Wall. 2017. *Governance for Peace: How Inclusive, Participatory and Accountable Institutions Promote Peace and Prosperity.* Cambridge: Cambridge University Press.
Giugale, Marcelo M. 2017. *Economic Development: What Everyone Needs to Know.* 2nd ed. Oxford: Oxford University Press.
Goldstein, Joshua S. 2011. *Winning the War on War: The Decline of Armed Conflict Worldwide.* New York: Dutton.
Hathaway, Oona A., and Scott J. Shapiro. 2017. *The Internationalists: How a Radical Plan to Outlaw War Remade the World.* New York: Simon & Schuster.
Hawksley, Theodora. 2020. *Peacebuilding and Catholic Social Teaching.* Notre Dame, IN: University of Notre Dame Press.
Hedges, Chris. 2002. *War Is a Force That Gives Us Meaning.* New York: Anchor Books.
Horgan, John. 2012. *The End of War.* San Francisco: McSweeney's Books.
Kenny, Charles. 2011. *Getting Better: Why Global Development Is Succeeding— And How We Can Improve the World Even More.* New York: Basic Books.
Lamb, Christina. 2020. *Our Bodies, Their Battlefields: War through the Lives of Women.* New York: Scribner.
Massaro, Thomas J., S.J., and Thomas A. Shannon. 2003. *Catholic Perspectives on War and Peace.* Lanham, MD: Rowman & Littlefield.
McCarthy, Eli S., ed. 2020. *A Just Peace Ethic Primer: Building Sustainable Peace and Breaking Cycles of Violence.* Washington, DC: Georgetown University Press.
O'Reilly, Marie. 2015. *Why Women: Inclusive Security and Peaceful Societies.* Washington, DC: Inclusive Security.
Popovic, Srdja. 2015. *Blueprint for Revolution: How to Use Rice Pudding, Lego Men, and Other Nonviolent Techniques to Galvanize Communities, Overthrow Dictators, or Simply Change the World.* New York: Spiegel & Grau.
Schlabach, Gerald W., ed. 2007. *Just Policing, Not War.* Collegeville, MN: Liturgical Press.
Slim, Hugo. 2008. *Killing Civilians: Method, Madness, and Morality in War.* New York: Columbia University Press.
Stassen, Glen H., ed. 2008. *Just Peacemaking: The New Paradigm for the Ethics of Peace and War.* New ed. Cleveland: Pilgrim Press.
Winright, Tobias, and Laurie Johnston, eds. 2015. *Can War Be Just in the 21st Century? Ethicists Engage the Tradition.* Maryknoll, NY: Orbis Books.

NOTES

INTRODUCTION

1. Paul VI 1966, p. 54; John Paul II 1991a, sec. 52; Francis 2013; 2020a, sec. 258.
2. John Paul II 2003a, p. 544.
3. For overviews of the development of just war theory in the Catholic and other Christian traditions, see Cahill 1994; Massaro and Shannon 2003.
4. Second Vatican Council 1965, sec. 80.
5. For overviews of these shifts, see Himes 1991, 2008; Duffey 1995; Massaro and Shannon 2003; Shadle 2011, chaps. 7–8; Cochran 2014a, chap. 4.
6. Stassen 2008; Berger et al. 2020; McCarthy 2020.
7. Second Vatican Council 1965, sec. 70; John Paul II 1991d; 1993a; 1995a, sec. 55; 2000, secs. 3 and 11; 2002, sec. 5; Pontifical Council for Justice and Peace 2004, sec. 504.
8. Pope Francis, quoted in Rocca 2014; Francis 2015a, sec. 200; 2020a, sec. 258, including n. 242.
9. Francis 2022a; Vatican News Staff 2022.
10. See, for example, two special issues of the journal *Expositions* (*Expositions* 2018; *Expositions* 2019).
11. See, for example, Neuhaus 2003; Weigel 2003, 2010; Schall 2004; Christiansen 2005; Patterson 2007.
12. I have previously developed particular elements of this overall argument in Cochran 2014a, 2014b, 2015, 2016, 2018, 2019, 2021.

CHAPTER I. War's Death, Destruction, and Dehumanization

1. John Paul II 1995a, secs. 3, 10, 19, 57; 2003a, p. 544; Benedict XVI 2007b, sec. 5.
2. Benedict XV 1914, sec. 3; Paul VI 1966, p. 54; John Paul II 1991a, sec. 52; 2000, sec. 3.
3. John Paul II 2000, sec. 12; Pontifical Council for Justice and Peace 2004, chap. 11; Francis 2019, sec. 6; 2020a, sec. 261; 2022a; Vatican News Staff 2022.
4. John Paul II 1996, sec. 2; see also Francis 2014a; 2020a, sec. 261.
5. John XXIII 1963, sec. 127; Second Vatican Council 1965, secs. 79–80; John Paul II 1991a, sec. 51; Francis 2015a, secs. 57, 104; 2020a, sec. 258.
6. "Pope on Hiroshima" 2020.
7. Augustine 1950, book 19, chaps. 13 and 17; John Paul II 2002, sec. 3.
8. John XIII 1963, secs. 8–10, 31–35, 46; Second Vatican Council 1965, sec. 26; John Paul II 1993b, sec. 1; Benedict XVI 2005, sec. 28; 2009a, sec. 78; Francis 2020a, sec. 235.
9. John XXIII 1963, sec. 34; Francis 2020b.
10. John XXIII 1963, sec. 48; Second Vatican Council 1965, sec. 78; Benedict XVI 2013, sec. 3; Francis 2019, sec. 6; 2020a, sec. 256.
11. Second Vatican Council 1965, sec. 77; Francis 2021, sec. 1.
12. For a good overview, see Pontifical Council for Justice and Peace 2004, chap. 11.
13. Francis 2021, sec. 7.
14. John Paul II 2000, sec. 3.
15. Paul VI 1966, p. 54; John Paul II 1993b, sec. 4; Francis 2015a; 2016, sec. 8.
16. Benedict XV, 1914, sec. 3; John Paul II 1987, sec. 24; 1994, secs. 3–5; 1996, secs. 2–4; Francis 2015b, sec. 4; 2018, secs. 1–2.
17. Francis 2014a; 2018, secs. 1–2; 2019, sec. 6; 2020a, sec. 261.
18. John Paul II 1993b, sec. 4; 1996, secs. 2–4; Francis 2014b, sec. 7; 2020a, sec. 261; 2020b, sec. 2; 2022b.

19. John Paul II 1993b, secs. 3–4; Benedict XVI 2009b, sec. 1; Francis 2020b, sec. 1.
20. Benedict XV 1914, sec. 3.
21. John Paul II 1993b, sec. 4.
22. John XXIII 1963, sec. 109; Second Vatican Council 1965, sec. 81; Paul VI 1967, sec. 51; John Paul II 1987, secs. 10, 21, 23; 1991a, sec. 28; Pontifical Council for Justice and Peace 1994; Benedict XVI 2008, sec. 14; 2009b, sec. 6; Francis 2017, sec. 2; 2020a, sec. 262; 2021, sec. 7.
23. John XXIII 1961, sec. 204; World Synod of Catholic Bishops 1971, sec. 9; Paul VI 1977, pp. 243–44; John Paul II 1991a, sec. 18; 2002, sec. 9.
24. John Paul II 1991a, sec. 52; 1993b, sec. 2; 2003a, p. 544.
25. Francis 2016, secs. 4 and 8; 2019, sec. 6; 2020b, sec. 1; 2022a.
26. Bourke 1999, xvii; Grossman 2009, 92.
27. Hallock 1999, 66; Kyle 2012, 253.
28. Hallock 1999, 156; Bourke 2006, 20; Wright 2006, 157; Sheehan 2008, 112; Pinker 2011, chap. 5 and p. 340.
29. Erasmus 1990a, 306.
30. Tirman 2011, chap. 10.
31. Walzer 1992, chap. 16; Hedges 2002, 95; Dyer 2004, chap. 5; Slim 2008, chap. 2; Shue 2010; Whitlock 2010; Tirman 2011.
32. LeBlanc and Register 2003, 67.
33. Potts and Hayden 2008, 245.
34. Sheehan 2008, 96.
35. Snyder 2010, 205–6.
36. Tirman 2011, 295.
37. Wright 2006, 304.
38. Keegan 1993, 171; LeBlanc and Register 2003, 199.
39. Slim 2008, chap. 3.
40. Bourke 2006, 21; Tirman 2011, 250; Winright 2011, 2015; Johnston 2015.
41. Kassimeris 2006; Potts and Hayden 2008, chaps. 7, 9; Slim 2008; Shue 2010.
42. Finkel 2009; Khatchadourian 2009; Tirman 2011, chap. 9.
43. Grossman 2009, 199–201.

44. Tirman 2011, 251.
45. Khatchadourian 2009; Filkins 2011; Tirman 2011, chap. 9.
46. Gopal 2020.
47. Slim 2008, 91.
48. Keegan 1993, 5; Dyer 2004, chap. 6; Slim 2008, 71; Pinker 2011, 67.
49. Holmes 1989, 6.
50. Goldstein 2011, chap. 10.
51. Hedges 2002, 13–14.
52. Tirman 2011.
53. Kinder and Kam 2009, 119–20.
54. Slim 2008, chaps. 1, 4, 5.
55. Bourke 1999, chap. 6; Sheehan 2008, 129; Aslan 2009, 103.
56. Hassan 2001, 38; Ackerman 2005, 18; Bourke 2006, 159; Mayer 2009, 31.
57. Anscombe 1970, 50–51; Ford 1970, 27–28; Johnstone 1986; Holmes 1989, 196–200; Bica 1999; Khatchadourian 2009, 53.
58. Holmes 1989, 46; Kassimeris 2006, 6; Slim 2008, chap. 3.
59. Erasmus 1972, 23.
60. Hallock 1999, 97.
61. Walzer 1992, chaps. 3, 9; Christopher 1999; Kahn 2002; McKeogh 2002, chap. 6.
62. Ratzinger 1998, 14–38; Allen 2000, 15–23; Bernstein and Landler 2005; Rising and Surman 2005; Sparks, Follain, and Morgan 2005.
63. LeBlanc and Register 2003, 67; Dyer 2004, chaps. 4–5; Grossman 2009, 70.
64. Boggs 2005, 181; Tirman 2011, 201.
65. Dyer 2004, 186, 221; Sheehan 2008, 75, 124; Batuman 2011.
66. LeBlanc and Register 2003, 62.
67. Keegan 1993, 171.
68. Erasmus 1990b, 280–81.
69. Blattman 2022, 11.
70. Hallock 1999; Hedges 2002; Dyer 2004; Peppard 2008; Sheehan 2008, chaps. 3–6; Slim 2008; Finkel 2009; Grossman 2009; Harr 2009;

Mujica 2011; Tirman 2011; Levinger 2013, chap. 1; Johnston 2015; Cortright, Seyle, and Wall 2017, 186–87; Giugale 2017, 24; Grayling 2017, chap. 5.
71. Hallock 1999, 340; Dyer 2004, 4.
72. Slim 2008, 60–61.
73. Bourke 1999, chap. 6; Slim 2008, chap. 2; Grossman 2009, sec. 5.
74. Lamb 2020.
75. Lamb 2020, 5, 81, 164, 169, 171, 174, 249.
76. Lamb 2020, 61, 274, 293–94.
77. Lamb 2020, 9, 82–83.
78. Lamb 2020, 89, 326–27.
79. Lamb 2020, 6–7.
80. Lamb 2020, 4, 7.
81. Lamb 2020, 147, 162–63, 290–99, 315, and chap. 5.
82. Hedges 2002, 139; Claiborne and Haw 2008, 216.
83. Bourke 1999, 355.
84. Dyer 2004, 30; Habeck 2006, 98; Potts and Hayden 2008, 253.
85. Dyer 2004, 31.
86. Bourke 1999, chaps. 3, 7; Hallock 1999, chap. 3; Kassimeris 2006; Slim 2008, chap. 6.
87. Grossman 2009, sec. 1.
88. Grossman 2009, 87.
89. Grossman 2009, 128, 178, 256–57, and secs. 2–4.
90. Tirman 2011, 296.
91. Bourke 1999, 25.
92. Dyer 2004, 154.
93. Bourke 1999, 19–20, 30.
94. Hallock 1999, 50.
95. Scahill 2008, 157.
96. Ferguson 2006, 152.
97. Weil 1977.
98. Bourke 1999, 193, 344; Dyer 2004, 18, 255; Lamb 2020, 154.
99. Bourke 1999; Hedges 2002, chaps. 2, 4; Potts and Hayden 2008; Slim 2008; Grossman 2009, sec. 5.

100. Erasmus 1972, 20; Hedges 2002, 101.

101. Bourke 1999, 171, 216, 355; Hallock 1999, 313; Dyer 2004, 248; Snyder 2010, 173.

CHAPTER 2. War's False Promises and the Power of Nonviolence

1. John Paul II 1991a, sec. 25; 2005, sec. 4.

2. Francis 2020a, secs. 258, 261, 282.

3. John XXIII 1963, secs. 110–11, 128–29; Second Vatican Council 1965, secs. 83, 86; Paul VI 1967, secs. 62–63; 1971, sec. 45; 1977; World Synod of Catholic Bishops 1971, sec. 3; John Paul II 1987, secs. 22, 37; 1991a, secs. 17–18, 27; Francis 2017, sec. 4; 2020a. secs. 30, 127, 262; 2020b, secs. 1–2; 2021, sec. 7.

4. John Paul II 1999, sec. 11.

5. John Paul II 1993b, sec. 4; 2002, sec. 10; 2005, sec. 4.

6. Francis 2017, sec. 2; 2020a, sec. 255; 2021, sec. 1; Vatican News Staff 2022.

7. John XXIII 1961, sec. 206; John Paul II 1991a, sec. 18; Francis 2020a, secs. 258, 262; 2020b, sec. 1; 2021, sec. 7.

8. Paul VI 1967, sec. 31; 1975, sec. 37; John Paul II 1991a, sec. 52; Francis 2020a, secs. 257, 261.

9. John Paul II 1991a, sec. 18; 1991c, pp. 534–35; 1993b, sec. 4; 2000, sec. 8; 2020a, sec. 249; 2020b, sec. 1; 2022b.

10. Second Vatican Council 1965, sec. 81; Paul VI 1975, sec. 37; John Paul II 1991c, p. 530; 1991b; 2000, sec. 3; Francis 2013; 2020a, secs. 227, 250–51, 259; 2020b, sec. 2.

11. John XXIII 1961, secs. 200–206; Paul VI 1966; World Synod of Catholic Bishops 1971, sec. 9; John Paul II 1987, sec. 24; 1991a, sec. 28; Pontifical Council for Justice and Peace 1994; Francis 2014b, sec. 7; 2017, sec. 2; 2019, sec. 6.

12. Second Vatican Council 1965, sec. 81; Paul VI 1977; John Paul II 1995a, sec. 10; 1999, sec. 11; Benedict XVI 2008, sec. 14; 2009b, sec. 6.

13. Second Vatican Council 1965, sec. 78; World Synod of Catholic Bishops 1971, sec. 65; Paul VI 1977; Pontifical Council for Justice and Peace 1994; Francis 2020a, secs. 243, 249.

14. John Paul II 1991a, sec. 23; 1995a, sec. 27; 2000, sec. 4; Benedict XVI 2007a; Francis 2017, secs. 1, 4, 6.
15. Hedges 2002, 3, 10, 46, 63, 149.
16. Hallock 1999, chap. 8; Hedges 2002, 142–43; Tirman 2011, chaps. 4, 5, 7.
17. Bourke 2006, 29; Kaplan 2011, 9; Lamb 2020, 93.
18. Bourke 1999; Scahill 2008, 33; Slim 2008; Grossman 2009, 37; Osborn 2011.
19. Tirman 2011, 121.
20. Thomsen 2011.
21. Bourke 1999, chap. 2; Hallock 1999; Hedges 2002, 3; Dyer 2004, 104–5; Finkel 2009.
22. Hallock 1999, 94–95.
23. Blincoe 2007.
24. Erasmus 1972, 19.
25. Gilbert 1947, 279; Osnos 2017, 49.
26. Anscombe 1970, 44.
27. Bacevich 2005, 2, 53, 97–98.
28. Bacevich 2005, 97; Scahill 2008, 194; Finkel 2009, 202, 213.
29. Bacevich 2005, 19, 97.
30. Cady 1989, preface; Holmes 1989, 12; Bacevich 2005, 18, 216–17.
31. Dyer 2004, 426.
32. Keegan 1993, 21; Sheehan 2008, 70–71.
33. Bacevich 2005, 3, 7, 147, 203.
34. Howard 2008; Kaplan 2008; Hari 2009.
35. Yoder 1992, 76.
36. Stoessinger 2005.
37. Keegan 1993, 21; Bacevich 2005; Kaplan 2008; Kaiser 2010; Lievan 2011; Tirman 2011, chap. 7; Allo 2021; Caesar 2021, 40; Coll and Entous 2021, 34.
38. Blattman 2022, chap. 6.
39. Blattman 2022, 11.
40. Sample 2002; Biddle 2004; Dyer 2004, 290; Bacevich 2005; Morgan 2006, chap. 4; Kaplan 2008; Ringsmose 2008; Rosenbaum 2010; Cortright, Seyle, and Wall 2017, 59, 65–66; Kaplan 2021.

41. Zunes 2017.

42. Fry 2007, 18–20; Horgan 2012, 128.

43. Sample 2002; Senese and Vasquez 2005; Asal and Beardsley 2007; Mitchell and Vasquez 2021, 335.

44. Feinstein 2016; Pamp et al. 2018; Mehri and Thurner 2020.

45. Stephan and Chenoweth 2008; Chenoweth and Stephan 2011; Chenoweth and Stephan 2016; Chenoweth 2021.

46. Chenoweth and Stephan 2011, 29 and chap. 8.

47. Chenoweth 2021, 241.

48. Chenoweth 2021, 208.

49. Shaw 2003; Valentino 2004; Slim 2008, chap. 2; Straus 2012; Levinger 2013, chap. 3; Klare 2016; Welsh 2016; Chenoweth and Perkoski 2017; Perkoski and Chenoweth 2018; Ackerman and Merriman 2019, 3–4; Chenoweth 2021, 197, 208, 217.

50. Evans 2008.

51. Chandler 2004; Seybolt 2007, chap. 1.

52. Regan 2000, chap. 6; Doyle and Sambanis 2006, 44; Paris 2014; Welsh 2016; Cortright, Seyle, and Wall 2017, 173–74.

53. Mégret 2009; Paris 2014; Luck and Luck 2016.

54. Kuperman 2008; 2009; Mégret 2009; Ackerman and Merriman 2019.

55. Seybolt 2007, chaps. 2–3; Newman 2009; Paris 2014; Conley-Zilkic 2016; House of Commons 2016.

56. Seybolt 2007.

57. House of Commons 2016.

58. Paris 2014; Kuperman 2015; Lamb 2020, 43; Walsh 2021.

59. Sharp 1990a, 22.

60. Sharp 1990a, 1990b, 2005; Schell 2003; Stephan and Chenoweth 2008; Chenoweth and Stephan 2011; Popovic 2015; Stephan 2020; Chenoweth 2021.

61. Ackerman and DuVall 2000; Chenoweth and Stephan 2016; Chenoweth 2021.

62. Stephan and Chenoweth 2008; Chenoweth and Stephan 2011; Chenoweth 2021.

63. Chenoweth and Stephan 2016; Chenoweth 2021, chap. 5.

64. Sharp and Jenkins 2003; Katatnycky and Ackerman 2005; Zunes 2017.

65. Chenoweth and Stephan 2011, 10.

66. Ackerman and DuVall 2000; Stephan and Chenoweth 2008; Chenoweth and Stephan 2011; Chenoweth and Stephan 2016; Stephan 2020, 145; Chenoweth 2021, 190, 214.

67. Chenoweth 2021, 95.

68. Chenoweth 2019; Stephan 2020; Chenoweth 2021, 94–100, 114–18.

69. Stephan and Chenoweth 2008, 42; Chenoweth 2013; Popovic 2015, chaps. 2, 3, 6; Stephan 2020, 144–45; Chenoweth 2021, 192–95 and chap. 1.

70. Stephan and Chenoweth 2008, 13; Chenoweth and Stephan 2011; Chenoweth 2021, chaps. 1–2.

71. Chenoweth and Stephan 2011, 29; Stephan 2020, 145; Chenoweth 2021, 89, 241.

72. Chenoweth and Stephan 2011, chap. 8; Chenoweth 2021, 243.

73. Celestino and Gleditsch 2013; Bayer, Bethke, and Lambach 2016; Bethke and Pinckney 2016; Zunes 2017; Pinckney 2018, 43.

74. Pinckney 2018; Chenoweth 2021, 241.

75. Chenoweth and Stephan 2011, 202; Chenoweth 2021, 241.

76. Chenoweth and Perkoski 2017; Perkoski and Chenoweth 2018; Ackerman and Merriman 2019, 6; Chenoweth 2021, 185, 190–91, 196–97, 208, 217.

77. Mégret 2009; Ackerman and Merriman 2019.

78. Coy 2012; Duncan and Ashworth 2020; Stephan 2020, 148; Chenoweth 2021, 219.

79. Mégret 2009.

80. Anderson and Wallace 2013; Kaplan 2017.

81. Anderson and Wallace 2013, 9.

82. Sémelin, Andrieu, and Gensburger 2014; Lamb 2020.

83. Arendt 1963, chaps. 10–11; Vassilev 2010; Wilcock 2012; Moorehead 2014; Snyder 2015; Mayersen 2016; Lamb 2020, chap. 6; Stephan 2020, 147; Chenoweth 2021, 204–7.

CHAPTER 3. Preventing War through Greater Global Governance

1. John XXIII 1961, secs. 200–206; Second Vatican Council 1965, secs. 23, 26; John Paul II 1987, sec. 26; 1991a, sec. 27; Benedict XVI 2009a, secs. 9, 33, 67; Francis 2020a, sec. 262.

2. John Paul II 1987, sec. 39; Benedict XVI 2009a, secs. 9, 33, 42; 2009b.

3. John XXIII 1963, sec. 132; Second Vatican Council 1965, secs. 24–25, 33, 54, 75, 77; John Paul II 1987, secs. 38, 45; 2000, sec. 6; Francis 2020a, secs. 30, 137.

4. John XXIII 1961, secs. 200–206; 1963, secs. 113, 118; Second Vatican Council 1965, sec. 82; Paul VI 1971, sec. 45; 1977; Francis 2013; 2014b, sec. 7; 2020a, sec. 175.

5. John XXIII 1961, secs. 200–206; 1963, secs. 98–99, 114; Second Vatican Council 1965, sec. 25; John Paul II 1987, sec. 22; 1991a, secs. 35, 51; Pontifical Council for Justice and Peace 2004, chap. 9; Francis 2014b, sec. 4; 2015a, secs. 164–69; 2016, sec. 2.

6. John Paul II 1987, sec. 39.

7. John XXIII 1963, sec. 139; Second Vatican Council 1965, sec. 84; Paul VI 1967, sec. 78; Benedict XVI 2009a, sec. 42.

8. John XXIII 1963, sec. 137.

9. John XXIII 1963, sec. 139; Second Vatican Council 1965, sec. 82; Paul VI 1967, sec. 78; John Paul II 2003b, sec. 6; Pontifical Council for Justice and Peace 2004, p. 441; Francis 2015a, sec. 175; 2020a, sec. 132.

10. Paul VI 1977; John Paul II 1987, sec. 43; 1991a, sec. 52; 2003b, sec. 5; Benedict XVI 2009a, sec. 41; Francis 2020a, sec. 172.

11. Benedict XVI 2009a, sec. 67.

12. John XXIII 1963, secs. 140–41; Paul VI 1977; John Paul II 2000, sec. 6; 2003b, sec. 6; Pontifical Council for Justice and Peace 2004, p. 435; Benedict XVI 2009a, secs. 24, 41, 67; Francis 2020a, sec. 231.

13. John XXIII 1961, sec. 49.

14. John XXIII 1963, secs. 103–8; Second Vatican Council 1965, secs. 83–84, 86, 90; Paul VI 1967, secs. 77–78; World Synod of Catholic Bishops 1971, secs. 66–71; John Paul II 1987, secs. 26, 45; 2000, secs. 10, 12; 2003a, pp. 544–45; 2004, sec. 7; Pontifical Council for Justice and Peace

2004, sec. 443; Benedict XVI 2009a, secs. 24–25, 71–72; 2010, sec. 14; Francis 2014b, sec. 7; 2016, secs. 2, 7; 2017, sec. 6; 2018, sec. 5; 2020a, secs. 172, 174–75, 231.

15. John XXIII 1963, sec. 80; John Paul II 1987, secs. 39, 43; 1991a, sec. 58; Francis 2014b, sec. 4.

16. Paul VI 1977, p. 248; John Paul II 1991c, pp. 530–31; 2000, sec. 12; 2003a, p. 544; 2004, sec. 6; Pontifical Council for Justice and Peace 2004, sec. 441; Benedict XVI 2008, secs. 11, 13; 2009a, sec. 67; Francis 2014b, sec. 7; 2021, sec. 7.

17. John XXIII 1963, sec. 144; Paul VI 1977; John Paul II 1987, sec. 26; Pontifical Council for Justice and Peace 1994; John Paul II 2000, sec. 7; 2004, secs. 5, 9; Pontifical Council for Justice and Peace 2004, sec. 506; Benedict XVI 2007b, sec. 13.

18. John XXIII 1963, secs. 142–45; Paul VI 1966; 1967, sec. 78; 1977; John Paul II 1987, sec. 26; 1991a, sec. 21; Pontifical Council for Justice and Peace 1994; John Paul II 2003b, sec. 5; Benedict XVI 2007b, sec. 13; 2009a, sec. 67.

19. John Paul II 2000, sec. 11; 2004, sec. 7; Francis 2020a, secs. 173, 257.

20. World Synod of Catholic Bishops 1971, sec. 65.

21. Benedict XVI 2008, sec. 14; John XXIII 1961, secs. 200–206; 1963, sec. 112; Second Vatican Council 1965, sec. 82; World Synod of Catholic Bishops 1971, sec. 65; Paul VI 1977; Pontifical Council for Justice and Peace 1994; John Paul II 1999, sec. 11; Francis 2014b, sec. 7; 2017, sec. 5; 2020a, sec. 262; 2021, sec. 7.

22. John XXIII 1963, secs. 93, 118, 126, 129; Second Vatican Council 1965, secs. 84, 88; Paul VI 1971, sec. 43; World Synod of Catholic Bishops 1971, sec. 65; John Paul II 1991a, secs. 21, 27–28, 51; 1999, sec. 11; Pontifical Council for Justice and Peace 1994; John Paul II 2000, sec. 8; Benedict XVI 2009a, secs. 71–72; Francis 2014b, sec. 7; 2016, sec. 8; 2018, sec. 5; 2020a, secs. 173–74, 231, 257.

23. Finnemore 2003, 3, 17.

24. Wendt 1992; Katzenstein 1996; Wendt 1999, 20, 310–11; Finnemore 2003.

25. Wendt 1992; Katzenstein 1996; Wendt 1999; Finnemore 2003, 4–5.

26. Keohane 1984; Toulmin 1992; Katzenstein 1996; Keohane 2001; Morgan 2006, chap. 8; Cortright, Seyle, and Wall 2017, 46–47, 229–31, 246; Blattman 2022, chap. 9.

27. Keohane 1984; Nadelmann 1990; Toulmin 1992, 287–88; Wendt 1999, 361; Andreas and Nadelmann 2006; Morgan 2006, chap. 9; Cortright 2007; Winright 2007; Lopez 2008; Levinger 2013; Lopez 2016; Blattman 2022, chap. 10.

28. Russett and Oneal 2001; Morgan 2006, chap. 8; Cortright 2007; Sheehan 2008; Pinker 2011, chaps. 5–6; Cortright, Seyle, and Wall 2017, 201–5, 232–33; Blattman 2022, chap. 7.

29. Pape 2006; Wright 2006; Jones and Libicki 2008, xvii; Sageman 2008; Aslan 2009; Berman 2009; Cronin 2009; Pape and Feldman 2010; Lamb 2020, chap. 12.

30. Hamm 2007, 16; Jones and Libicki 2008; Rosen 2008; Sageman 2008; Aslan 2009; Lamb 2020, chap. 3; Saiya 2021.

31. Cortright, Seyle, and Wall 2017, 17.

32. Price and Tannenwald 1996; Morgan 2006; Green and Stassen 2008; Keefe 2010; Goldstein 2011, 18; Pinker 2011, 272–73; Winright 2011; Feinstein 2016; Cortright, Seyle, and Wall 2017, 248.

33. Hathaway and Shapiro 2017, xiv, xv, 42–43, 91.

34. Hathaway and Shapiro 2017, xii, 128.

35. Hathaway and Shapiro 2017, xiv, 314.

36. Hathaway and Shapiro 2017, xii, 311, 314, and chap. 13.

37. Hathaway and Shapiro 2017, chap. 16.

38. Cortright 2007; Wallensteen 2007, chap. 9; Lopez 2008; Escribà-Folch 2010; Lopez 2016; Blattman 2022, chaps. 9–10.

39. Levinger 2013, 54–55.

40. Kupchan 2010.

41. Russett and Oneal 2001, 40; Morgan 2006, chap. 9; Sampson 2007; Goldstein 2011, 188–89; Weigand and Powell 2011; Marazziti 2012; Blattman 2022, chap. 10.

42. Bremer 1992; Ramsbotham, Woodhouse, and Miall 2005, chap. 4; Morgan 2006, chap. 9; Wallensteen 2007, 259–66; Levinger 2013, chap. 3; Mitchell and Vasquez 2021, chap. 19; Blattman 2022.

43. Crocker, Hampson, and Aall 2004; Ramsbotham, Woodhouse, and Miall 2005, chap. 4; Morgan 2006, chap. 9; Bercovitch 2007; Wallensteen 2007; Brion-Meisels et al. 2008; Levinger 2013, chap. 2; Hampson and Zartman 2015; Blattman 2022, chaps. 5, 10.

44. Bilder 2007; Wallensteen 2007; Goldstein 2011, 191.

45. Wallensteen 2007, 88, 266; Goldstein 2011, 191; Blattman 2022, chap. 10.

46. Keegan 1993, 386; Mueller 2004, 31–32; Anderson and Wallace 2013; Blattman 2022, 11.

47. Berger 1996; Jervis 2002; Mueller 2004, 67, 82–84; Senese and Vasquez 2005; Morgan 2006, 163; Wallensteen 2007, 158–59; Hensel et al. 2008; Goldstein 2011, 6, 237, 278–79; Mitchell and Vasquez 2021, 220–27, 333.

48. Ray 1989, 432–33; Wendt 1999, 289; Mueller 2004; Ramsbotham, Woodhouse, and Miall 2005; Morgan 2006, chap. 8; Sheehan 2008; Cortright, Seyle, and Wall 2017, 2.

49. Cortright, Seyle, and Wall 2017, x, 12, and chap. 10.

50. Mueller 2004; Ramsbotham, Woodhouse, and Miall 2005, chaps. 7, 9; Doyle and Sambanis 2006, 11; Collier 2007, 27; Wallensteen 2007, chap. 4; Collier 2008, 104; Hewitt, Wilkenfeld, and Gurr 2010, 1; Goldstein 2011, 279–80; Levinger 2013, chap. 2; Cortright, Seyle, and Wall 2017, 236.

51. Paffenholz 2013.

52. Crocker, Hampson, and Aall 2004; Wallensteen 2007, chap. 9; Escribà-Folch 2010; Goldstein 2011; Cortright, Seyle, and Wall 2017, 141.

53. Dobbins et al. 2005; Doyle and Sambanis 2006, 46; Dobbins 2007; Wallensteen 2007, chap. 2; Hewitt, Wilkenfeld, and Gurr 2010, chap. 7; Goldstein 2011; Cortright, Seyle, and Wall 2017, 240–41; Blattman 2022, chap. 10.

54. Cortright, Seyle, and Wall 2017, 240.

55. Dobbins et al. 2005; Ramsbotham, Woodhouse, and Miall 2005, chaps. 4, 8; Doyle and Sambanis 2006; Morgan 2006, chap. 10; Dobbins 2007; Wallensteen 2007, chaps. 6, 9; Goldstein 2011; Blattman 2022, chaps. 5, 10.

56. Mueller 2004, 1, 15; Ramsbotham, Woodhouse, and Miall 2005, chap. 6; Dobbins et al. 2007; Wallensteen 2007, 148; Jensen 2008; Rubin 2008; Levinger 2013, chap. 2; Cortright, Seyle, and Wall 2017, 99, 140.

57. Wallensteen 2007, 245; Goldstein 2011, 7 and chap. 7.

58. Dobbins et al. 2005; Ramsbotham, Woodhouse, and Miall 2005, chap. 8; Doyle and Sambanis 2006; Morgan 2006, chap. 10; Dobbins 2007; Goldstein 2011, 310–12.

59. Hewitt, Wilkenfeld, and Gurr 2010, chap. 9; O'Reilly 2015; Stephan 2020, 151.

60. Wallensteen 2007; Odendaal 2013; Cortright, Seyle, and Wall 2017, 43, 247–48.

61. Anderson and Wallace 2013; Dudouet 2017.

62. Bellamy 2016; Leaning 2016; Mayersen 2016.

63. Chirot and McCauley 2006; Feinstein 2016; Klare 2016; Lopez 2016; Luck and Luck 2016; Welsh 2016.

64. Pell and Bonner 2016.

CHAPTER 4. Preventing War through Economic and Political Justice

1. Second Vatican Council 1965, secs. 78, 83; Paul VI 1967, sec. 76; 1972; 1977; John Paul II 1991a, sec. 18; 1993b, sec. 1; Francis 2015a, sec. 225.

2. Second Vatican Council 1965, secs. 1–2, 40–45, 55, 77; World Synod of Catholic Bishops 1971, secs. 3, 5–6; Paul VI 1975, sec. 36; John Paul II 1995a, sec. 36; Benedict XVI 2005, sec. 28; 2009a, sec. 78; Francis 2019, sec. 7.

3. John XXIII 1963, secs. 8–27, 31–36; Second Vatican Council 1965, secs. 26–27; World Synod of Catholic Bishops 1971, sec. 63; John Paul II 1993b, sec. 1.

4. Second Vatican Council 1965, sec. 26.

5. Paul VI 1975, sec. 36; John Paul II 1987, sec. 39; 1991a, sec. 18; 2002, sec. 2; Benedict XVI 2009a, sec. 78; Francis 2020a, sec. 116; 2020b, sec. 2.

6. Second Vatican Council 1965, sec. 83; John Paul II 1991a, secs. 27, 52; Pontifical Council for Justice and Peace 1994; John Paul II 2002,

sec. 5; Pontifical Council for Justice and Peace 2004, secs. 513–14; Benedict XVI 2009b, sec. 6; Francis 2016, sec. 4.

7. Paul VI 1967, sec. 76; John Paul II 1987, sec. 39; 1991a, sec. 52.

8. John XXIII 1963, sec. 64; Second Vatican Council 1965, sec. 88; Paul VI 1967, sec. 9; World Synod of Catholic Bishops 1971, sec. 16; John Paul II 1987, secs. 14–15, 19, 22, 28, 39, 42; 1993b, secs. 1, 3–4; 1995a, sec. 10; Benedict XVI 2009a, secs. 22, 17, 29; 2009b, secs. 1, 6; 2013, secs. 1, 5; Francis 2014b, sec. 5; 2020b, sec. 2.

9. World Synod of Catholic Bishops 1971, secs. 66–71; John Paul II 1987, sec. 27; 1991a, secs. 28, 52, 58; Benedict XVI 2009a, secs. 41–42.

10. John XXIII 1963, secs. 64, 122–23; Second Vatican Council 1965, secs. 31, 72; Paul VI 1966; 1967, sec. 33; 1971, sec. 46; World Synod of Catholic Bishops 1971, secs. 13, 15; John Paul II 1987, sec. 35; 1991a, secs. 19, 35; 1998, sec. 6; Benedict XVI 2009a, secs. 27, 61, 65–66; 2013, secs. 4–5; Francis 2014b, sec. 5; 2020a, secs. 116, 126.

11. John XXIII 1961, secs. 157–74; Second Vatican Council 1965, sec. 88; Paul VI 1967, secs. 52, 58–59; John Paul II 1987, secs. 17, 21, 26, 32; 1991a, secs. 52, 58; Benedict XVI 2009a, secs. 21–22, 25, 47, 58–60, 67; 2009b, sec. 12; 2010, sec. 7.

12. Paul VI 1971, sec. 21; John Paul II 1987, secs. 26, 28, 34; 1990; 1991a, secs. 36–37, 52; 1995a, sec. 10; Pontifical Council for Justice and Peace 2004, chap. 10; Benedict XVI 2009a, secs. 21, 27, 32, 48–52; 2010; Francis 2015a; 2016, sec. 2.

13. Paul VI 1967, secs. 14, 20, 34, 47; John Paul II 1987, secs. 1, 15, 28–30, 33; 1991a, sec. 29; Benedict XVI 2009a, secs. 11, 18, 23, 67; Francis 2020a, sec. 235.

14. John XXIII 1963, secs. 48, 61; Second Vatican Council 1965, secs. 73–76; Paul VI 1967, sec. 30; World Synod of Catholic Bishops 1971, secs. 9, 22–26; John Paul II 1987, sec. 15; 1991a, secs. 29, 44–45; 1999, sec. 1; Pontifical Council for Justice and Peace 2004, chap. 3; Benedict XVI 2008, sec. 11; Francis 2020a, sec. 235.

15. John XXIII 1963, secs. 52, 54; Second Vatican Council 1965, secs. 73–74; John Paul II 1987, sec. 43; 1991a, sec. 22; 1991c; Pontifical Council on Justice and Peace 1994; John Paul II 2003b, sec. 4; Pontifical Council for Justice and Peace 2004, chap. 3; Benedict XVI 2009a, secs. 21, 41; 2013, sec. 5.

16. John XXIII 1963, secs. 67–79, 94–97, 122–23; Second Vatican Council 1965, secs. 31, 73–76; Paul VI 1967, secs. 30, 33–35; 1971, secs. 24, 41; World Synod of Catholic Bishops 1971, secs. 39–58; John Paul II 1987, secs. 33, 43; 1991a, secs. 17, 44, 46; 1998, sec. 5; 2003b, sec. 8; 2004, sec. 8; Pontifical Council for Justice and Peace 2004, chap. 3; Benedict XVI 2008, secs. 11–13; 2009a, secs. 32, 41, 57; Francis 2014b, sec. 7; 2020b, sec. 2.

17. John XXIII 1963, secs. 11–27, 39–43, 60–61, 75, 94–97, 142–45; Second Vatican Council 1965, secs. 29, 60, 73–76; Paul VI 1966; 1967, secs. 10, 34–35; 1971, sec. 13; World Synod of Catholic Bishops 1971, secs. 15, 21–22, 39–58, 63; John Paul II 1987, secs. 33, 43; 1989; 1991a, sec. 29; 1991c, p. 530; 1995b; 1999, sec. 1; 2003b, secs. 4, 6; Pontifical Council for Justice and Peace 2004, chap. 3; Benedict XVI 2007b, secs. 7, 12–13; Francis 2020b, sec. 2.

18. Cortright, Seyle, and Wall 2017, 4, 15.

19. Bremer 1992; Stewart 2002; Doyle and Sambanis 2006, chap. 2; Collier 2007, chap. 2; Cortright 2007; Goldstein 2011, chap. 11; Pinker 2011, chaps. 5, 6; Cortright, Seyle, and Wall 2017, 18–21, 96, 181–82, 201–5, 217–19; Giugale 2017, 26–32; Blattman 2022, chap. 7.

20. Stewart 2002; Cortright, Seyle, and Wall 2017, 18, 36–37, 185–86.

21. O'Reilly 2015; Cortright, Seyle, and Wall 2017, 19 and chap. 5; Giugale 2017, 89–97.

22. Cortright, Seyle, and Wall 2017, 18, 77, 84, 118, 181–82; Giugale 2017, 89–97.

23. LeBlanc and Register 2003; Pinker 2011, 376; Horgan 2012, chap. 3; Levinger 2013, chap. 3; Gleditsch 2015, 150–53; Welzer 2017; Mach et al. 2019.

24. Bryant and Kappaz 2005, chap. 4; Sachs 2005; Collier 2007; Cortright, Seyle, and Wall 2017, 20–21, 77, 96, 180–81, 187, 201–10; Giugale 2017, 39, 162–63; Twilley 2022.

25. Bryant and Kappaz 2005, chap. 4; Sachs 2005; Cohen and Easterly 2009; Cortright, Seyle, and Wall 2017, 5, 9, 20–21, 219–21.

26. Giugale 2017, 38, 71–72, 76–77, 81, 103.

27. Potts and Hayden 2008, 366; Cortright, Seyle, and Wall 2017, 14, 77, 118, 181, 79, and chap. 3; Giugale 2017, 79–80.

28. Collier 2007, chap. 2; Cortright, Seyle, and Wall 2017, 18, 217–19; Giugale 2017, 26–32, 51–52, 71–72.

29. Weaver, Rock, and Kusterer 1997; Bryant and Kappaz 2005; Cortright, Seyle, and Wall 2017, 20–21, 75; Giugale 2017, 1, 67.

30. O'Reilly 2015; Cortright, Seyle, and Wall 2017, 19, 112, 115, 120–21; Giugale 2017, 79–80, 89, 94, 96–97.

31. Gourevitch 1998; Riddell 2007; Moyo 2009; Fisman 2012; Giugale 2017, 83–84, 156–60.

32. Bryant and Kappaz 2005, chap. 4; Sachs 2005; Riddell 2007; Cohen and Easterly 2009; Banerjee and Duflo 2011; Cortright, Seyle, and Wall 2017, 191; Giugale 2017, 80, 154–160.

33. Bryant and Kappaz 2005, chap 4; Moyo 2009, 133–36.

34. Gleditsch 2015, 153; Giugale 2017, 190–93; Diffenbaugh and Burke 2019.

35. Bryant and Kappaz 2005; Cheema 2005; Sachs 2005; Collier 2007; Acemoglu and Robinson 2012; Haugen and Boutros 2014; Cortright, Seyle, and Wall 2017.

36. Cortright, Seyle, and Wall 2017, x, 15.

37. Rummel 1997; Hegre et al. 2001; Cortright 2007; Wallensteen 2007, chap. 6; Gleditsch and Ruggeri 2010; Goldstein 2011; Pinker 2011, chaps. 5–6; Hegre 2014; Cortright, Seyle, and Wall 2017, 7, 108–9, 160–64, 170–71, 176; Bartusevičius and Skaaning 2018; Saiya 2021.

38. Doyle 1986; Bremer 1992; Russett 1993; Rummel 1997; Ward and Gleditsch 1998; Russett and Oneal 2001; Russett 2008; Hegre 2014; Cortright, Seyle, and Wall 2017, 7, 19, 157; Mitchell and Vasquez 2021.

39. Ward and Gleditsch 1998; Hegre et al. 2001; Mansfield and Snyder 2005; Pinker 2011, 310; Cortright, Seyle, and Wall 2017, 7, 167–69.

40. Cheema 2005; Wallensteen 2007, 109; Diamond 2008a, 2008b; Sørensen 2008, chap. 4; Wittes 2008; Hook 2010; McFaul 2010, chap. 5; Stephan, Lakhani, and Naviwala 2015; Cortright, Seyle, and Wall 2017, 260–61; Pinckney 2018; Ackerman and Merriman 2019; Chenoweth 2021, 136–38, 192–93, 219–20, 243; Blattman 2022, chap. 8.

41. Mansfield and Snyder 2005; McFaul 2010, chap. 5.

42. Gurr 2000; Stewart 2002; Chirot and McCauley 2006; Doyle and Sambanis 2006, chap. 2; Collier 2007, chap. 2; Wallensteen 2007, 123, 167,

172; Acemoglu and Robinson 2012; Cortright, Seyle, and Wall 2107, 8–9, 14, 16, 18, 20, 78, 86, 93–94, 97, 100–101, 105–8, 165–67; Pinckney 2018; Blattman 2022, chap. 8.

43. Gurr 2000; Uvin 2004; Cheema 2005, chap. 5; Zakaria 2007; Cortright, Seyle, and Wall 2017, 163, 174–75.

44. O'Reilly 2015; Cortright, Seyle, and Wall 2017, 19, 113–21.

45. Varshney 2002; Diamond 2008b; Cortright, Seyle, and Wall 2017, 8–9, 16, 37–39, 196.

46. Diamond 2008b; Cortright, Seyle, and Wall 2017, 12–14, 29, 174.

47. Mueller 2004, 1, 172; Diamond 2008a; Glenny 2008; Anderson 2009; Goldstein 2011, chap. 11; Acemoglu and Robinson 2012.

48. Cheema 2005, chap. 8; Carothers 2006; Power 2008; Banerjee and Duflo 2011, 235–37, 245–49; Cortright, Seyle, and Wall 2017, 7, 9, 12–13, 17, 31, 58–61, 76–77, 139; Giugale 2017, 22–23, 25, 101–2; Blattman 2022, chap 2.

49. Wallensteen 2007, 276; Cortright, Seyle, and Wall 2017, 19, 130, 139.

50. Cheema 2005, chap. 3; McFaul 2010, 202–3; Banerjee and Duflo 2011, 244–45, 253; Cortright, Seyle, and Wall 2017, chap. 6; Giugale 2017, 22–23, 84, 168–71.

51. Haugen and Boutros 2014.

52. Giugale 2017, 63.

53. Acemoglu and Robinson 2012; Cortright, Seyle, and Wall 2017, 21, 162–63, 206–10, 215–19; Giugale 2017, 26–32, 51–52, 63.

54. Dobbins et al. 2007, chap. 9; Collier 2008; Hewitt, Wilkenfeld, and Gurr 2010, chap. 7; Goldstein 2011, 106; Cortright, Seyle, and Wall 2017, 17.

55. Mueller 2004; Dobbins et al. 2007, chaps. 3–4, 6–7; Carnahan and Lockhart 2008; Jensen 2008; Rubin 2008; Cortright, Seyle, and Wall 2017, 145.

56. Ramsbotham, Woodhouse, and Miall 2005, chaps. 8–10; Doyle and Sambanis 2006, 342–45; Morgan 2006, chap. 12; Dobbins et al. 2007, chap. 8; Wallensteen 2007, 272–79; Hewitt, Wilkenfeld, and Gurr 2010, chaps. 8, 10; Olsen, Payne, and Reiter 2010, chap. 7; Demeritt, Nichols, and Kelly 2014, 362; O'Reilly 2015; Cortright, Seyle, and Wall 2017, 13, 106–8, 160, 166, 240; Pinckney 2018.

CHAPTER 5. Abolishing War

1. Paul VI 1966, p. 54; John Paul II 1991a, sec. 52; Francis 2013; 2020a, sec. 258.
2. Second Vatican Council 1965, sec. 81; John Paul II 1982, sec. 2; 1991c, p. 531; Francis 2014b, sec. 7; 2014a; 2022b.
3. Second Vatican Council 1965, sec. 79; Paul VI 1977; John Paul II 1991a, sec. 52.
4. Second Vatican Council 1965, sec. 25; World Synod of Catholic Bishops 1971, secs. 5, 16; John Paul II 1984, sec. 16; 1987, secs. 16, 36–39; 1995a, sec. 12; *Catechism of the Catholic Church* 1997, sec. 1869; Francis 2015a, sec. 66.
5. Paul VI 1975, sec. 36; John Paul II 1984, sec. 16; 1987, sec. 37; 1991a, sec. 38; 1995a, sec. 29.
6. Francis 2022b.
7. Second Vatican Council 1965, secs. 25, 40; Paul VI 1975, sec. 36; John Paul II 1987, secs. 25, 47; Benedict XVI 2009a, sec. 34.
8. Second Vatican Council 1965, secs. 29, 33–39, 55, 57, 77; World Synod of Catholic Bishops 1971, sec. 6; John Paul II 1987, sec. 47; 1991a, secs. 25–26; 1995a, sec. 6; Benedict XVI 2009a, sec. 7.
9. John XXIII 1963, sec. 162; Second Vatican Council 1965, secs. 29–30, 53, 73; Benedict XVI 2009a, sec. 78.
10. Paul VI 1967, sec. 79; John Paul II 1987, sec. 47; 1991a, sec. 25; Benedict XVI 2009a, sec. 21; 2013, sec. 3; Francis 2017, sec. 3; 2020a, secs. 127, 261.
11. John Paul II 1987, sec. 31.
12. John XXIII 1963, secs. 39–43; Second Vatican Council 1965, secs. 31, 40–45, 54–55, 73, 77; Paul VI 1967, secs. 12, 15–17, 34–35, 43, 79; 1971, secs. 41, 45; World Synod of Catholic Bishops, 1971, secs. 7–14; John Paul II 1987, sec. 38; 1991a, sec. 21; 1991c, p. 531; 1995a, sec. 26; 2000, sec. 8; Benedict XVI 2006, secs. 12–14; 2009b, sec. 3; Francis 2020a, sec. 256.
13. Francis 2015b, sec. 3.
14. Augustine 1950, book 19, chap. 15; O'Connell 2017; Griffiths 2017; Francis 2020a, secs. 255, 263–70; Martin 2020.

15. Mead 2006, 218–19, 221.
16. Mead 2006, 221.
17. Fry 2007, 2; 2013, 4.
18. Mueller 2004, 31–32; Malinowski 2006; Fry 2007; Horgan 2012; Fry 2013; Grayling 2017, chap. 4.
19. Keegan 1993, 121, 251, 266.
20. Megivern 1997; Banner 2002, 114, 116, and chap. 4; Cawthorne 2006.
21. Banner 2002, 106, 125–27, and chaps. 4–5.
22. Bae 2007, 1.
23. Bartlett 1986, 2, 9–10, 110; Kiernan 1988, chaps. 2–3.
24. Bartlett 1986, 77, 105.
25. Kiernan 1988, 122; Holland 2003, 51, 75, 83, 115, 118, 147.
26. Kiernan 1988, 138 and chap. 2; Holland 2003, 142; Mead 2006, 220; Spierenburg 2008, 76 and chap 3; Norris 2009, 94, 111–12; Roth 2009, 160; Appiah 2010, 36.
27. Kiernan 1988, 63, 82, 136–37, 272; Spierenburg 2008, 73; Appiah 2010, chap 1.
28. Kiernan 1988, 11; Holland 2003, 5–6, 150; Spierenburg 2008, chap. 3; Norris 2009, 35.
29. Patterson 1982; Keegan 1993, 343; Davis 1998, ix; Patterson 1999, ix; Davis 2006, 107–9, 118–19, 201.
30. Augustine 1950, book 19, chap. 15; Aristotle 1986, 22; Fitzhugh 1998, 275, 277; Davis 1999, 208.
31. Davis 1966, 396; 1984, 23; 2006, 80.
32. Davis 1999, 345; 2006, 285, 317, 325.
33. Bae 2007.
34. Bartlett 1986, chaps. 5–7; Kiernan 1988, chap. 3.
35. Kiernan 1988, 218 and chaps. 10, 12; Spierenburg 2008, chaps. 3, 6; Norris 2009, 68 and chap. 10; Appiah 2010, chap. 1.
36. Davis 1984, 108; 1999, 15, 48; 2006, chap. 6 and p. 142; Appiah 2010, chap. 3.
37. Davis 1999; Metaxas 2007; Chenoweth 2021, 20.
38. Nadelmann 1990; Davis 2014.

39. Ray 1989; Nadelmann 1990; Andreas and Nadelmann 2006; Appiah 2010, chap. 3; Davis 2014.

40. Davis 1984, part 3, chap. 3; Waldrep 2002; Dray 2003; Davis 2014.

41. Douglas 1986, 45, 47–48, 91, 114.

42. Mueller 2004, chap. 2 and p. 84; Pinker 2011, 242–43. The quotations from de Tocqueville, Hegel, and Stravinsky are in Pinker 2011.

43. Keegan 1993, 58–59; Stoessinger 2005, 309–10; Cortright 2008.

44. Pinker 2011, chaps. 5–6; 2018, chap. 11; Braumoeller 2019.

45. Jervis 2002, 1; Mueller 2004, 67, 83–84; Senese and Vasquez 2005; Hensel et al. 2008.

46. Goldstein 2011, chap. 2; Brown and Stewart 2015, 200–201; Center for Systemic Peace; Roser et al. 2016; Uppsala Conflict Data Program website.

47. Pinkovskiy and Sala-i-Martin 2010; Kenny 2011c; 2011a; 2011b, 9, 77, 80; Cortright, Seyle, and Wall 2017, 198; Giugale 2017, 55, 70, 163; Estes and Sirgy 2018, 237–40; United Nations Development Programme.

48. Diamond 2008a; Sørensen 2008, chap. 2; Cortright, Seyle, and Wall 2017, 169, 175–76; Applebaum 2020; Repucci and Slipowitz 2022; Center for Systemic Peace.

49. John Paul II 2005, sec. 11.

WORKS CITED

VATICAN DOCUMENTS AND PAPAL STATEMENTS

Benedict XV. 1914. *Ad Beatissimi Apostolorum.* https://www.vatican.va/content/benedict-xv/en/encyclicals/documents/hf_ben-xv_enc_01111914_ad-beatissimi-apostolorum.html.

Benedict XVI. 2005. *Deus Caritas Est.* https://www.vatican.va/content/benedict-xvi/en/encyclicals/documents/hf_ben-xvi_enc_20051225_deus-caritas-est.html.

———. 2006. *World Day of Peace Message.* http://www.vatican.va/holy_father/benedict_xvi/messages/peace/documents/hf_ben-xvi_mes_20051213_xxxix-world-day-peace_en.html.

———. 2007a. *Angelus.* https://www.vatican.va/content/benedict-xvi/en/angelus/2007/documents/hf_ben-xvi_ang_20070218.html.

———. 2007b. *World Day of Peace Message.* http://www.vatican.va/holy_father/benedict_xvi/messages/peace/documents/hf_ben-xvi_mes_20061208_xl-world-day-peace_en.html.

———. 2008. *World Day of Peace Message.* http://www.vatican.va/holy_father/benedict_xvi/messages/peace/documents/hf_ben-xvi_mes_20071208_xli-world-day-peace_en.html.

———. 2009a. *Caritas in Veritate.* http://www.vatican.va/holy_father/benedict_xvi/encyclicals/documents/hf_ben-xvi_enc_20090629_caritas-in-veritate_en.html.

———. 2009b. *World Day of Peace Message.* http://www.vatican.va/holy_father/benedict_xvi/messages/peace/documents/hf_ben-xvi_mes_20081208_xlii-world-day-peace_en.html.

———. 2010. *World Day of Peace Message.* http://www.vatican.va/holy_father/benedict_xvi/messages/peace/documents/hf_ben-xvi_mes_20091208_xliii-world-day-peace_en.html.

———. 2013. *World Day of Peace Message.* http://www.vatican.va/holy_father/benedict_xvi/messages/peace/documents/hf_ben-xvi_mes_20121208_xlvi-world-day-peace_en.html.

Catechism of the Catholic Church. 1997. 2nd ed. Vatican City: Libreria Editrice Vaticana.

Francis. 2013. *Angelus.* https://www.vatican.va/content/francesco/en/angelus/2013/documents/papa-francesco_angelus_20130901.html.

———. 2014a. *Angelus.* https://www.vatican.va/content/francesco/en/angelus/2014/documents/papa-francesco_angelus_20140727.html.

———. 2014b. *World Day of Peace Message.* https://www.vatican.va/content/francesco/en/messages/peace/documents/papa-francesco_20131208_messaggio-xlvii-giornata-mondiale-pace-2014.html.

———. 2015a. *Laudato Si.* https://www.vatican.va/content/francesco/en/encyclicals/documents/papa-francesco_20150524_enciclica-laudato-si.html.

———. 2015b. *World Day of Peace Message.* https://www.vatican.va/content/francesco/en/messages/peace/documents/papa-francesco_20141208_messaggio-xlviii-giornata-mondiale-pace-2015.html.

———. 2016. *World Day of Peace Message.* https://www.vatican.va/content/francesco/en/messages/peace/documents/papa-francesco_20151208_messaggio-xlix-giornata-mondiale-pace-2016.html.

———. 2017. *World Day of Peace Message.* https://www.vatican.va/content/francesco/en/messages/peace/documents/papa-francesco_20161208_messaggio-l-giornata-mondiale-pace-2017.html.

———. 2018. *World Day of Peace Message.* https://www.vatican.va/content/francesco/en/messages/peace/documents/papa-francesco_20171113_messaggio-51giornatamondiale-pace2018.html.

———. 2019. *World Day of Peace Message.* https://www.vatican.va/content/francesco/en/messages/peace/documents/papa-francesco_20181208_messaggio-52giornatamondiale-pace2019.html.

———. 2020a. *Fratelli Tutti.* https://www.vatican.va/content/francesco/en/encyclicals/documents/papa-francesco_20201003_enciclica-fratelli-tutti.html.

———. 2020b. *World Day of Peace Message*. https://www.vatican.va/content/francesco/en/messages/peace/documents/papa-francesco_20191208_messaggio-53giornatamondiale-pace2020.html.

———. 2021. *World Day of Peace Message*. https://www.vatican.va/content/francesco/en/messages/peace/documents/papa-francesco_20201208_messaggio-54giornatamondiale-pace2021.html.

———. 2022a. *Address of His Holiness Pope Francis to Participants in the International Congress Promoted by the Pontifical Foundation Gravissimum Educationis*. https://www.vatican.va/content/francesco/en/speeches/2022/march/documents/20220318-fondazione-gravissimum-educationis.html.

———. 2022b. *Angelus*. https://www.vatican.va/content/francesco/en/angelus/2022/documents/20220327-angelus.html.

John XXIII. 1961. *Mater et Magistra*. http://www.vatican.va/holy_father/john_xxiii/encyclicals/documents/hf_j-xxiii_enc_15051961_mater_en.html.

———. 1963. *Pacem in Terris*. http://www.vatican.va/holy_father/john_xxiii/encyclicals/documents/hf_j-xxiii_enc_11041963_pacem_en.html.

John Paul II. 1982. *Homily at Holy Mass of Pentecost*. https://www.vatican.va/content/john-paul-ii/en/homilies/1982/documents/hf_jp-ii_hom_19820530_coventry.html.

———. 1984. *Reconciliation and Penance*. http://www.vatican.va/holy_father/john_paul_ii/apost_exhortations/documents/hf_jp-ii_exh_02121984_reconciliatio-et-paenitentia_en.html.

———. 1987. *Sollicitudo rei Socialis*. http://www.vatican.va/holy_father/john_paul_ii/encyclicals/documents/hf_jp-ii_enc_30121987_sollicitudo-rei-socialis_en.html.

———. 1989. *World Day of Peace Message*. http://www.vatican.va/holy_father/john_paul_ii/messages/peace/documents/hf_jp-ii_mes_19881208_xxii-world-day-for-peace_en.html.

———. 1990. *World Day of Peace Message*. http://www.vatican.va/holy_father/john_paul_ii/messages/peace/documents/hf_jp-ii_mes_19891208_xxiii-world-day-for-peace_en.html.

———. 1991a. *Centesimus Annus*. http://www.vatican.va/holy_father/john_paul_ii/encyclicals/documents/hf_jp-ii_enc_01051991_centesimus-annus_en.html.

———. 1991b. "The Pope's Letters to Bush and Hussein." *Origins* 20 (33): 534–35.

———. 1991c. "War, a Decline for Humanity." *Origins* 20 (33): 525–31.

———. 1991d. "We Are Not Pacifists." *Origins* 20 (36): 625.

———. 1993a. "Principles Underlying a Stance toward Unjust Aggressors." *Origins* 22 (34): 583–87.

———. 1993b. *World Day of Peace Message.* http://www.vatican.va/holy_father/john_paul_ii/messages/peace/documents/hf_jp-ii_mes_08121992_xxvi-world-day-for-peace_en.html.

———. 1994. *World Day of Peace Message.* http://www.vatican.va/holy_father/john_paul_ii/messages/peace/documents/hf_jp-ii_mes_08121993_xxvii-world-day-for-peace_en.html.

———. 1995a. *Evangelium Vitae.* http://www.vatican.va/holy_father/john_paul_ii/encyclicals/documents/hf_jp-ii_enc_25031995_evangelium-vitae_en.html.

———. 1995b. *World Day of Peace Message.* http://www.vatican.va/holy_father/john_paul_ii/messages/peace/documents/hf_jp-ii_mes_08121994_xxviii-world-day-for-peace_en.html.

———. 1996. *World Day of Peace Message.* http://www.vatican.va/holy_father/john_paul_ii/messages/peace/documents/hf_jp-ii_mes_08121995_xxix-world-day-for-peace_en.html.

———. 1998. *World Day of Peace Message.* http://www.vatican.va/holy_father/john_paul_ii/messages/peace/documents/hf_jp-ii_mes_08121997_xxxi-world-day-for-peace_en.html.

———. 1999. *World Day of Peace Message.* http://www.vatican.va/holy_father/john_paul_ii/messages/peace/documents/hf_jp-ii_mes_14121998_xxxii-world-day-for-peace_en.html.

———. 2000. *World Day of Peace Message.* http://www.vatican.va/holy_father/john_paul_ii/messages/peace/documents/hf_jp-ii_mes_08121999_xxxiii-world-day-for-peace_en.html.

———. 2002. *World Day of Peace Message.* http://www.vatican.va/holy_father/john_paul_ii/messages/peace/documents/hf_jp-ii_mes_20011211_xxxv-world-day-for-peace_en.html.

———. 2003a. "The International Situation Today." *Origins* 32 (33): 543–45.

———. 2003b. *World Day of Peace Message.* http://www.vatican.va/holy_father/john_paul_ii/messages/peace/documents/hf_jp-ii_mes_20021217_xxxvi-world-day-for-peace_en.html.

———. 2004. *World Day of Peace Message.* http://www.vatican.va/holy
_father/john_paul_ii/messages/peace/documents/hf_jp-ii_mes_2003
1216_xxxvii-world-day-for-peace_en.html.

———. 2005. *World Day of Peace Message.* http://www.vatican.va/holy
_father/john_paul_ii/messages/peace/documents/hf_jp-ii_mes_2004
1216_xxxviii-world-day-for-peace_en.html.

Paul VI. 1966. "Address of Pope Paul VI to the UN General Assembly." *The Pope Speaks* 11 (1): 47–57.

———. 1967. *Populorum Progressio.* http://www.vatican.va/holy_father
/paul_vi/encyclicals/documents/hf_p-vi_enc_26031967_populorum
_en.html.

———. 1971. *Octogesima Adveniens.* http://www.vatican.va/holy_father
/paul_vi/apost_letters/documents/hf_p-vi_apl_19710514_octogesima
-adveniens_en.html.

———. 1972. *World Day of Peace Message.* https://www.vatican.va/content
/paul-vi/en/messages/peace/documents/hf_p-vi_mes_19711208
_v-world-day-for-peace.html.

———. 1975. *Evangelii Nuntiandi.* http://www.vatican.va/holy_father
/paul_vi/apost_exhortations/documents/hf_p-vi_exh_19751208_evangelii
-nuntiandi_en.html.

———. 1977. "The Holy See and Disarmament." *The Pope Speaks* 22 (3): 243–59.

Pontifical Council for Justice and Peace. 1994. *The International Arms Trade: An Ethical Reflection.* Vatican City: Libreria Editrice Vaticana.

———. 2004. *Compendium of the Social Doctrine of the Church.* Washington, DC: United States Conference of Catholic Bishops.

"Pope on Hiroshima: Possession of Nuclear Weapons 'Immoral.'" 2020. *Washington Post*, August 6, 2020.

Rocca, Francis X. 2014. "Pope Talks Airstrikes in Iraq, His Health, Possible US Visit." *National Catholic Reporter*, August 18, 2014. https://www
.ncronline.org/news/world/pope-talks-airstrikes-iraq-his-health-possible
-us-visit.

Second Vatican Council. 1965. *Gaudium et Spes.* http://www.vatican.va
/archive/hist_councils/ii_vatican_council/documents/vat-ii_const
_19651207_gaudium-et-spes_en.html.

Vatican News Staff. 2022. "Pope to Russian Patriarch: 'Church Uses Language of Jesus, Not of Politics.'" *Vatican News*, March 16.

World Synod of Catholic Bishops. 1971. *Justice in the World*. Catholic Charities Twin Cities. https://www.cctwincities.org/wp-content/uploads/2015/10/Justicia-in-Mundo.pdf.

OTHER SOURCES

Acemoglu, Daron, and James Robinson. 2012. *Why Nations Fail: The Origins of Power, Prosperity, and Poverty*. New York: Crown.

Ackerman, Peter, and Jack DuVall. 2000. *A Force More Powerful: A Century of Nonviolent Conflict*. New York: Palgrave.

Ackerman, Peter, and Hardy Merriman. 2019. *Preventing Mass Atrocities: From a Responsibility to Protect (RtoP) to a Right to Assist (RtoA) Campaigns of Civil Resistance*. Washington, DC: International Center on Nonviolent Conflict.

Ackerman, Spencer. 2005. "Religious Protection." *New Republic*, December 12.

Allen, John L., Jr. 2000. *Pope Benedict XVI: A Biography of Joseph Ratzinger*. New York: Continuum.

Allo, Awol. 2021. "Ethiopia Is Spiraling, and There's One Man's Mistake behind It." *New York Times*, November 12.

Anderson, John Lee. 2009. "The Most Failed State." *New Yorker*, December 14.

Anderson, Mary B., and Marshall Wallace. 2013. *Opting Out of War: Strategies to Prevent Violent Conflict*. Boulder, CO: Lynne Rienner Publishers.

Andreas, Peter, and Ethan Nadelmann. 2006. *Policing the Globe: Criminalization and Crime Control in International Relations*. Oxford: Oxford University Press.

Anscombe, Elizabeth. 1970. "War and Murder." In *War and Morality*, edited by Richard A. Wasserstrom, 42–53. Belmont, CA: Wadsworth.

Appiah, Kwame Anthony. 2010. *The Honor Code: How Moral Revolutions Happen*. New York: W.W. Norton.

Applebaum, Anne, 2020. *Twilight of Democracy: The Seductive Lure of Authoritarianism*. New York: Doubleday.

Arendt, Hannah. 1963. *Eichmann in Jerusalem: A Report on the Banality of Evil*. New York: Penguin Books.

Aristotle. 1986. *Politics*. Translated by Hippocrates G. Apostle and Lloyd P. Gerson. Grinnell, IA: Peripatetic Press.

Asal, Victor, and Kyle Beardsley. 2007. "Proliferation and International Crisis Behavior." *Journal of Peace Research* 44 (2): 139–55.

Aslan, Reza. 2009. *How to Win a Cosmic War: God, Globalization, and the End of the War on Terror*. New York: Random House.

Augustine. 1950. *The City of God*. Translated by Marcus Dods, D.O. New York: Modern Library.

Bacevich, Andrew J. 2005. *The New American Militarism: How Americans Are Seduced by War*. Oxford: Oxford University Press.

Bae, Sangmin. 2007. *When the State No Longer Kills: International Human Rights Norms and the Abolition of Capital Punishment*. Albany: State University of New York Press.

Banerjee, Abhijit V., and Esther Duflo. 2011. *Poor Economics: A Radical Rethinking of the Way to Fight Global Poverty*. New York: Public Affairs.

Banner, Stuart. 2002. *The Death Penalty: An American History*. Cambridge, MA: Harvard University Press.

Bartlett, Robert. 1986. *Trial by Fire and Water: The Medieval Judicial Ordeal*. Oxford: Oxford University Press.

Bartusevičius, Henrikas, and Svend-Erik Skaaning. 2018. "Revisiting Democratic Civil Peace: Electoral Regimes and Civil Conflict." *Journal of Peace Research* 55 (5): 625–40.

Batuman, Elif. 2011. "Natural Histories." *New Yorker*, November 24.

Bayer, Markus, Felix S. Bethke, and Daniel Lambach. 2016. "The Democratic Dividend of Nonviolent Resistance." *Journal of Peace Research* 53 (6): 758–71.

Bellamy, Alex J. 2016. "Operationalizing the 'Atrocity Prevention Lens': Making Prevention a Living Reality." In Rosenberg, Galis, and Zucker, *Reconstructing Atrocity Prevention*, 61–80.

Bercovitch, Jacob. 2007. "Mediation in International Conflicts: Theory, Practice, and Developments." In Zartman, *Peacemaking in International Conflict*, 163–94.

Berger, Rose Marie, Ken Butigan, Judy Coode, and Marie Dennis, eds. 2020. *Advancing Nonviolence and Just Peace in the Church and the World*. Brussels: Pax Christi International.

Berger, Thomas U. 1996. "Norms, Identity, and National Security in Germany and Japan." In *The Culture of National Security: Norms and Identity in World Politics*, edited by Peter J. Katzenstein, 317–56. New York: Columbia University Press.

Berman, Eli. 2009. *Radical, Religious, and Violent: The New Economics of Terrorism.* Cambridge, MA: MIT Press.

Bernstein, Richard, and Mark Landler. 2005. "Few See Taint in Service by Pope in Hitler Youth." *New York Times*, April 21.

Bethke, Felix S., and Jonathan Pinckney. 2016. *Nonviolent Resistance and the Quality of Democracy.* Users Working Paper Series 2016, 03. Gothenburg: Varieties of Democracy Institute, University of Gothenburg.

Bica, Camillo C. 1999. "Another Perspective on the Doctrine of Double Effect." *Public Affairs Quarterly* 13 (2): 131–39.

Biddle, Stephen D. 2004. *Military Power: Explaining Victory and Defeat in Modern Battle.* Princeton: Princeton University Press.

Bilder, Richard D. 2007. "Adjudication: International Arbitral Tribunals and Courts." In Zartman, *Peacemaking in International Conflict*, 195–226.

Blattman, Christopher. 2022. *Why We Fight: The Roots of War and the Paths to Peace.* New York: Viking.

Blincoe, Nicholas. 2007. "His Words Liveth for Evermore." *Guardian*, November 11.

Boggs, Carl. 2005. *Imperial Delusions: American Militarism and Endless War.* Lanham, MD: Rowman & Littlefield.

Bourke, Joanna. 1999. *An Intimate History of Killing: Face to Face Killing in 20th Century Warfare.* New York: Basic Books.

———. 2006. "Barbarisation vs. Civilization in Time of War." In Kassimeris, *Barbarization of Warfare*, 19–38.

Braumoeller, Bear F. 2019. *Only the Dead: The Persistence of War in the Modern Age.* Oxford: Oxford University Press.

Bremer, Stuart A. 1992. "Dangerous Dyads: Conditions Affecting the Likelihood of Interstate War, 1816–1965." *Journal of Conflict Resolution* 36 (2): 309–41.

Brion-Meisels, Steven, Meenakshi Chhabra, David Cortright, David Steele, Gary Gunderson, and Edward LeRoy Long, Jr. 2008. "Use Cooperative Conflict Resolution." In Stassen, *Just Peacemaking*, 71–97.

Brown, Graham K., and Frances Stewart. 2015. "Economic and Political Causes of Conflict: An Overview and Some Polity Implications." In Crocker, Hampson, and Aall, *Managing Conflict in a World Adrift*, 199–227.

Bryant, Coralie, and Christina Kappaz. 2005. *Reducing Poverty, Building Peace*. Bloomfield, CT: Kumarian Press.

Cady, Duane L. 1989. *From Warism to Pacifism: A Moral Continuum*. Philadelphia: Temple University Press.

Caesar, Ed. 2021. "The Dead Ship." *New Yorker*, October 11.

Cahill, Lisa Sowle. 1994. *Love Your Enemies: Discipleship, Pacifism, and Just War Theory*. Minneapolis: Fortress.

Call, Charles T., and Vanessa Wyeth, eds. *Building States to Build Peace*. Boulder, CO: Lynne Rienner Publishers.

Carnahan, Michael, and Clare Lockhart. 2008. "Peacebuilding and Public Finance." In Call and Wyeth, *Building States to Build Peace*, 73–102.

Carothers, Thomas, ed. 2006. *Promoting the Rule of Law Abroad: In Search of Knowledge*. Washington, DC: Carnegie Endowment for International Peace.

Cawthorne, Nigel. 2006. *Public Executions: From Ancient Rome to the Present Day*. Edison, NJ: Chartwell Books.

Celestino, Mauricio Rivera, and Kristian Skrede Gleditsch. 2013. "Fresh Carnations or All Thorn, No Rose? Nonviolent Campaigns and Transitions in Autocracies." *Journal of Peace Research* 50 (3): 385–400.

Center for Systemic Peace. N.d. "Global Conflict Trends." https://www.systemicpeace.org/conflicttrends.html.

Chandler, David. 2004. "The Responsibility to Protect? Imposing the 'Liberal Peace.'" *International Peacekeeping* 11 (1): 59–81.

Cheema, G. Shabbir. 2005. *Building Democratic Institutions: Governance Reform in Developing Countries*. Bloomfield, CT: Kumarian Press.

Chenoweth, Erica. 2013. "The Success of Nonviolent Civil Resistance." YouTube video, 12:33. TEDx Boulder. November 4. https://www.youtube.com/watch?v=YJSehRlU34w.

———. 2019. *Women's Participation and the Fate of Nonviolent Campaigns: A Report on the Women in Resistance (WIRE) Data Set*. Broomfield, CO: One Earth Future Foundation.

———. 2021. *Civil Resistance: What Everyone Needs to Know*. Oxford: Oxford University Press.

Chenoweth, Erica, and Evan Perkoski. 2017. *Preventing Mass Atrocities*. Korbel Quickfacts in Peace and Security. Denver, CO: University of Denver Sie Cheou-Kang Center.

Chenoweth, Erica, and Maria J. Stephan. 2011. *Why Civil Resistance Works: The Strategic Logic of Nonviolent Conflict*. New York: Columbia University Press.

———. 2016. "How the World Is Proving Martin Luther King Right about Nonviolence." *Washington Post*, January 18.

Chirot, Daniel, and Clark McCauley. 2006. *Why Not Kill Them All? The Logic and Prevention of Mass Political Murder*. Princeton: Princeton University Press.

Christiansen, Drew, S.J. 2005. "Commentary on *Pacem in Terris* (*Peace on Earth*)." In *Modern Catholic Social Teaching: Commentaries and Interpretations*, edited by Kenneth R. Himes, O.F.M., 217–43. Washington, DC: Georgetown University Press.

Christopher, Paul. 1999. *The Ethics of War and Peace: An Introduction to Legal and Moral Issues*. 2nd ed. Upper Saddle River, NJ: Prentice Hall.

Claiborne, Shane, and Chris Haw. 2008. *Jesus for President: Politics for Ordinary Radicals*. Grand Rapids, MI: Zondervan.

Cochran, David Carroll. 2014a. *Catholic Realism and the Abolition of War*. Maryknoll, NY: Orbis Books.

———. 2014b. "War and the Surprising Realism of Catholicism's Peacemaking Agenda." *Journal of Catholic Social Thought* 11 (1): 105–25.

———. 2015. "What Slavery, Ordeals, Duels, and Lynching Can Teach us about Abolishing War." *Waging Nonviolence*, May 8.

———. 2016. "A World without War: Why It's No Fantasy." *Commonweal*, January 8.

———. 2018. "The Hidden Success of the 1928 Peace Pact." *Waging Nonviolence*, July 26.

———. 2019. "The Realism Objection to Setting Aside Just War Theory: A Response." *Expositions* 13 (2): 27–44.

———. 2021. "After 9/11 and Afghanistan, Does Just War Theory Have a Place in Catholic Thought?" *America*, September 16.

Cohen, Jessica, and William Easterly, eds. 2009. *What Works in Development: Thinking Big and Thinking Small*. Washington, DC: Brookings Institution Press.

Coll, Steve, and Adam Entous. 2021. "The Fall of the Islamic Republic." *New Yorker*, December 20.

Collier, Paul. 2007. *The Bottom Billion: Why the Poorest Countries Are Failing and What Can Be Done about It*. Oxford: Oxford University Press.

———. 2008. "Postconflict Economic Policy." In Call and Wyeth, *Building States to Build Peace*, 103–17.

Conley-Zilkic, Bridget. 2016. "The Pistol on the Wall: How Coercive Military Intervention Limits Atrocity Prevention." In Rosenberg, Galis, and Zucker, *Reconstructing Atrocity Prevention*, 31–60.

Cortright, David. 2007. "Sanctions and Stability Pacts: The Economic Tools of Peacemaking." In Zartman, *Peacemaking in International Conflict*, 385–418.

———. 2008. *Peace: A History of Movements and Ideas*. Cambridge: Cambridge University Press.

Cortright, David, Conor Seyle, and Kristen Wall. 2017. *Governance for Peace: How Inclusive, Participatory and Accountable Institutions Promote Peace and Prosperity*. Cambridge: Cambridge University Press.

Coy, Patrick G. 2012. "Nonpartisanship, Interventionism, and Legality in Accompaniment: Comparative Analysis of Peace Brigades International, Christian Peacemaker Teams, and the International Solidarity Movement." *International Journal of Human Rights* 16 (7): 963–81.

Crocker, Chester A., Fen Osler Hampson, and Pamela Aall, eds. 2015. *Managing Conflict in a World Adrift*. Washington, DC: United States Institute of Peace Press.

Crocker, Chester A., Fen Osler Hampson, and Pamela Aall. 2004. *Taming Interstate Conflicts: Mediation in the Hardest Cases*. Washington, DC: United States Institute of Peace Press.

Cronin, Audrey Kurth. 2009. *How Terrorism Ends: Understanding the Decline and Demise of Terrorist Campaigns*. Princeton: Princeton University Press.

Davis, David Brion. 1966. *The Problem of Slavery in Western Culture*. Oxford: Oxford University Press.

———. 1984. *Slavery and Human Progress*. Oxford: Oxford University Press.

———. 1998. "The Problem of Slavery." Introduction to *A Historical Guide to World Slavery*, edited by Seymour Drescher and Stanley L. Engerman. Oxford: Oxford University Press.

———. 1999. *The Problem of Slavery in the Age of Revolution, 1770–1823*. New ed. Oxford: Oxford University Press.

———. 2006. *Inhuman Bondage: The Rise and Fall of Slavery in the New World*. Oxford: Oxford University Press.

———. 2014. *The Problem of Slavery in the Age of Emancipation*. New York: Knopf.

Demeritt, Jacqueline H. R., Angela D. Nichols, and Eliza G. Kelly. 2014. "Female Participation and Civil War Relapse." *Civil War* 16 (3): 346–68.

Diamond, Larry. 2008a. "The Democratic Rollback." *Foreign Affairs* 87 (2): 36–48.

———. 2008b. *The Spirit of Democracy: The Struggle to Build Free Societies throughout the World*. New York: Henry Holt.

Diffenbaugh, Noah S., and Marshall Burke. 2019. "Global Warming Has Increased Global Economic Inequality." *PNAS* 116 (20): 9808–13.

Dobbins, James. 2007. *Testimony: A Comparative Evaluation of United Nations Peacekeeping*. Santa Monica, CA: RAND Corporation.

Dobbins, James, Seth G. Jones, Keith Crane, and Beth Cole DeGrasse. 2007. *The Beginner's Guide to Nation-Building*. Santa Monica, CA: RAND Corporation.

Dobbins, James, Seth G. Jones, Keith Crane, Andrew Rathmell, Brett Steele, Richard Teltschik, and Anga R. Timilsina. 2005. *The UN's Role in Nation Building: From the Congo to Iraq*. Santa Monica, CA: RAND Corporation.

Douglas, Mary. 1986. *How Institutions Think*. Syracuse, NY: Syracuse University Press.

Doyle, Michael W. 1986. "Liberalism and World Politics." *American Political Science Review* 80 (4): 1151–63.

Doyle, Michael W., and Nicholas Sambanis. 2006. *Making War and Building Peace: United Nations Peace Operations*. Princeton: Princeton University Press.

Dray, Philip. 2003. *At the Hands of Persons Unknown: The Lynching of Black America.* New York: Modern Library.

Dudouet, Véronique. 2017. *Powering to Peace: Integrated Civil Resistance and Peacebuilding Strategies.* Washington, DC: International Center on Nonviolent Conflict.

Duffey, Michael K. 1995. *Peacemaking Christians: The Future of Just Wars, Pacifism, and Nonviolent Resistance.* Kansas City: Sheed & Ward.

Duncan, Mel, and John Ashworth. 2020. "Living Just Peace in South Sudan: Protecting People Nonviolently in the Midst of War." In McCarthy, *Just Peace Ethic Primer*, 157–74.

Dyer, Gwynne. 2004. *War: The Lethal Custom.* Rev. ed. New York: Carroll & Graf.

Erasmus, Desiderius. 1972. "An Essay on War." In *Bellum: Two Statements on the Nature of War*, edited by William Royall Tyler. Barre, MA: Imprint Society.

———. 1990a. "A Complaint of Peace." In *The Erasmus Reader*, ed. Erika Rummel, 288–314. Toronto: University of Toronto Press.

———. 1990b. "The Education of a Christian Prince." In *The Erasmus Reader*, edited by Erika Rummel, 249–87. Toronto: University of Toronto Press.

Escribà-Folch, Abel. 2010. "Economic Sanctions and the Duration of Civil Conflicts." *Journal of Peace Research* 47 (2): 129–41.

Estes, Richard J., and M. Joseph Sirgy. 2018. *Advances in Well-Being: Towards a Better World.* London: Rowman & Littlefield.

Evans, Gareth. 2008. *The Responsibility to Protect: Ending Mass Atrocity Crimes Once and for All.* Washington, DC: Brookings Institution Press.

Expositions. 2018. Vol. 12, no. 1.

Expositions. 2019. Vol. 13, no. 2.

Feinstein, Andrew. 2016. "Through the Barrel of a Gun: Can Information from the Global Arms Trade Contribute to Genocide Prevention?" In Rosenberg, Galis, and Zucker, *Reconstructing Atrocity Prevention*, 196–206.

Ferguson, Niall. 2006. "Prisoner Taking and Prisoner Killing: The Dynamics of Defeat, Surrender and Barbarity in the Age of Total War." In Kassimeris, *Barbarization of Warfare*, 126–58.

Filkins, Dexter. 2011. "The Journalist and the Spies." *New Yorker*, September 19.

Finkel, David. 2009. *The Good Soldiers*. New York: Farrar, Straus and Giroux.

Finnemore, Martha. 2003. *The Purpose of Intervention: Changing Beliefs about the Use of Force*. Ithaca, NY: Cornell University Press.

Fisman, Ray. 2012. "Food for Naught: Does Sending Food Aid to Struggling Nations Do More Harm Than Good?" *Slate*, February 1.

Fitzhugh, George. 1998. "Cannibals All!" In *American Political Thought*, 4th ed., edited by Kenneth M. Dolbeare, 271–80. Chatham, NJ: Chatham House Publishers.

Ford, John C., S.J. 1970. "The Morality of Obliteration Bombing." In *War and Morality*, edited by Richard A. Wasserstrom, 15–41. Belmont, CA: Wadsworth.

Fry, Douglas P. 2007. *Beyond War: The Human Potential for Peace*. Oxford: Oxford University Press.

———, ed. 2013. *War, Peace, and Human Nature: The Convergence of Evolutionary and Cultural Views*. Oxford: Oxford University Press.

Gilbert, G. M. 1947. *Nuremberg Diary*. New York: Farrar, Straus.

Giugale, Marcelo M. 2017. *Economic Development: What Everyone Needs to Know*. 2nd ed. Oxford: Oxford University Press.

Gleditsch, Kristian Skrede, and Andrea Ruggeri. 2010. "Political Opportunity Structures, Democracy, and Civil War." *Journal of Peace Research* 47 (3): 299–310.

Gleditsch, Nils Petter. 2015. "Climate Change, Environmental Stress, and Conflict." In Crocker, Hampson, and Aall, *Managing Conflict in a World Adrift*, 147–68.

Glenny, Misha. 2008. *McMafia: A Journey through the Global Criminal Underworld*. New York: Knopf.

Goldstein, Joshua S. 2011. *Winning the War on War: The Decline of Armed Conflict Worldwide*. New York: Dutton.

Gopal, Anand. 2020. "America's War on Syrian Civilians." *New Yorker*, December 14.

Gourevitch, Philip. 1998. *We Wish To Inform You That Tomorrow We Will Be Killed with Our Families: Stories from Rwanda*. New York: Picador.

Grayling, A. C. 2017. *War: An Inquiry*. New Haven: Yale University Press.

Green, Barbara, and Glen Stassen. 2008. "Reduce Offensive Weapons and Weapons Trade." In Stassen, *Just Peacemaking*, 177–200.

Griffiths, Paul J. 2017. "Against Capital Punishment." *First Things*, December.
Grossman, Dave. 2009. *On Killing: The Psychological Cost of Learning to Kill in War and Society*. Rev. ed. New York: Little, Brown.
Gurr, Ted Robert. 2000. *Peoples Versus States: Minorities at Risk in the New Century*. Washington, DC: United States Institute of Peace Press.
Habeck, Mary R. 2006. "The Modern and the Primitive: Barbarity and Warfare on the Eastern Front." In Kassimeris, *Barbarization of Warfare*, 83–100.
Hallock, Dan. 1999. *Bloody Hell: The Price Soldiers Pay*. Farmington, PA: Plough Publishers.
Hamm, Mark S. 2007. *Terrorism as Crime: From Oklahoma City to Al-Qaeda and Beyond*. New York: New York University Press.
Hampson, Fen Osler, and I. William Zartman. 2015. "The Tools of Negotiation." In Crocker, Hampson, and Aall, *Managing Conflict in a World Adrift*, 377–95.
Hari, Johann. 2009. "Renouncing Islamism: To the Brink and Back Again." *Independent* (London), November 16.
Harr, Jonathan. 2009. "Lives of the Saints." *New Yorker*, January 5.
Hassan, Nasra. 2001. "An Arsenal of Believers." *New Yorker*, November 19.
Hathaway, Oona A., and Scott J. Shapiro. 2017. *The Internationalists: How a Radical Plan to Outlaw War Remade the World*. New York: Simon & Schuster.
Haugen, Gary A., and Victor Boutros. 2014. *The Locust Effect: Why the End of Poverty Requires the End of Violence*. Oxford: Oxford University Press.
Hedges, Chris. 2002. *War Is a Force That Gives Us Meaning*. New York: Anchor Books.
Hegre, Håvard. 2014. "Democracy and Armed Conflict." *Journal of Peace Research* 51 (2): 159–72.
Hegre, Håvard, Tanja Ellingsen, Scott Gates, and Nils Petter Gleditsch, 2001. "Toward A Democratic Civil Peace? Democracy, Political Change, and Civil War, 1816–1992." *American Political Science Review* 95 (1): 33–48.
Hensel, Paul R., Sara McLaughlin Mitchell, Thomas E. Sowers II, and Clayton L. Thyne. 2008. "Bones of Contention: Comparing Territorial, Maritime, and River Issues." *Journal of Conflict Resolution* 52 (1): 117–43.
Hewitt, J. Joseph, Jonathan Wilkenfeld, and Ted Robert Gurr. 2010. *Peace and Conflict 2010*. Boulder, CO: Paradigm Publishers.

Himes, Kenneth R., O.F.M. 1991. "Pacifism and the Just War Tradition in Roman Catholic Social Teaching." In *One Hundred Years of Catholic Social Thought: Celebration and Challenge*, edited by John A. Coleman, S.J., 329–44. Maryknoll, NY: Orbis Books.

———. 2008. "Working for Peace." In *We Hold These Truths: Catholicism and American Political Life*, edited by Richard W. Miller, 63–74. Liguori, MO: Liguori Publications.

Holland, Barbara. 2003. *Gentleman's Blood: A History of Dueling from Swords at Dawn to Pistols at Dusk*. New York: Bloomsbury.

Holmes, Robert L. 1989. *On War and Morality*. Princeton: Princeton University Press.

Hook, Steven W. 2010. *Democratic Peace in Theory and Practice*. Kent, OH: Kent State University Press.

Horgan, John. 2012. *The End of War*. San Francisco: McSweeney's Books.

House of Commons. 2016. *Libya: Examination of Intervention and Collapse and the UK's Future Policy Options*. London: House of Commons Foreign Affairs Committee.

Howard, Michael. 2008. *War and the Liberal Conscience*. New York: Columbia University Press.

Jensen, Erik G. 2008. "Justice and the Rule of Law." In Call and Wyeth, *Building States to Build Peace*, 119–42.

Jervis, Robert. 2002. "Theories of War in an Era of Leading-Power Peace." *American Political Science Review* 96 (1): 1–14.

Johnston, Laurie. 2015. "Just War Theory and Environmental Destruction." In *Can War Be Just in the 21st Century? Ethicists Engage the Tradition*, edited by Tobias Winright and Laurie Johnston, 96–111. Maryknoll, NY: Orbis Books.

Johnstone, Brian. 1986. "Noncombatant Immunity and the Prohibition of the Killing of the Innocent." In *Peace in a Nuclear Age: The Bishops' Pastoral Letter in Perspective*, edited by Charles J. Reid, Jr., 305–22. Washington, DC: Catholic University of America Press.

Jones, Seth G., and Martin C. Libicki. 2008. *How Terrorist Groups End: Lessons for Countering al Qa'ida*. Santa Monica, CA: RAND Corporation.

Kahn, Paul W. 2002. "The Paradox of Riskless Warfare." *Philosophy & Public Policy Quarterly* 22 (3): 2–8.

Kaiser, David. 2010. "Absurd, or Worse." *Commonweal*, March 12.

Kaplan, Fred. 2008. *Daydream Believers: How a Few Grand Ideas Wrecked American Power.* Hoboken, NJ: John Wiley & Sons.

———. 2021. "Does 'Deterrence' Work?" *Slate,* July 7.

Kaplan, Lawrence. 2011. "Vietnamization." *New Republic,* March 24.

Kaplan, Oliver. 2017. *Resisting War: How Communities Protect Themselves.* Cambridge: Cambridge University Press.

Kassimeris, George. 2006. "The Barbarisation of War: A User's Manual." In Kassimeris, *Barbarization of Warfare,* 1–18.

Kassimeris, George, ed. 2006. *The Barbarization of Warfare.* New York: New York University Press.

Katatnycky, Adrian, and Peter Ackerman. 2005. *How Freedom Is Won: From Civic Resistance to Durable Democracy.* Washington, DC: Freedom House.

Katzenstein, Peter J., ed. 1996. *The Culture of National Security: Norms and Identity in World Politics.* New York: Columbia University Press.

Keefe, Patrick Radden. 2010. "The Trafficker." *New Yorker,* February 8.

Keegan, John. 1993. *A History of Warfare.* New York: Vintage Books.

Kenny, Charles. 2011a. "Club for Growth." *Foreign Policy,* October 24.

———. 2011b. *Getting Better: Why Global Development Is Succeeding—And How We Can Improve the World Even More.* New York: Basic Books.

———. 2011c. "The Price Is Right." *Foreign Policy,* July 18.

Keohane, Robert O. 1984. *After Hegemony: Cooperation and Discord in the World Political Economy.* Princeton: Princeton University Press.

———. 2001. "Governance in a Partially Globalized World." *American Political Science Review* 95 (1): 1–13.

Khatchadourian, Raffi. 2009. "The Kill Company." *New Yorker,* July 6 and 13.

Kiernan, V. G. 1988. *The Duel in European History: Honour and the Reign of Aristocracy.* Oxford: Oxford University Press.

Kinder, Donald R., and Cindy D. Kam. 2009. *US against THEM: Ethnocentric Foundations of American Opinion.* Chicago: University of Chicago Press.

Klare, Michael T. 2016. "Resource Predation, Contemporary Conflict, and the Prevention of Genocide and Mass Atrocities." In Rosenberg, Galis, and Zucker, *Reconstructing Atrocity Prevention,* 249–76.

Kupchan, Charles A. 2010. *How Enemies Become Friends: The Sources of Stable Peace.* Princeton: Princeton University Press.

Kuperman, Alan J. 2008. "The Moral Hazard of Humanitarian Intervention: Lessons from the Balkans." *International Studies Quarterly* 52 (1): 49–80.

———. 2009. "Rethinking the Responsibility to Protect." *Whitehead Journal of Diplomacy and International Relations* 10 (1): 33–43.

———. 2015. "Obama's Libya Debacle." *Foreign Affairs* 94 (2): 66–77.

Kyle, Chris. 2012. *American Sniper: The Autobiography of the Most Lethal Sniper in U.S. Military History*. New York: HarperCollins.

Lamb, Christina. 2020. *Our Bodies, Their Battlefields: War through the Lives of Women*. New York: Scribner.

Leaning, Jennifer. 2016. "Early Warning for Mass Atrocities: Tracking Escalation Parameters at the Population Level." In Rosenberg, Galis, and Zucker, *Reconstructing Atrocity Prevention*, 352–78.

LeBlanc, Steven A., and Katherine E. Register. 2003. *Constant Battles: Why We Fight*. New York: St. Martin's Press.

Levinger, Matthew. 2013. *Conflict Analysis: Understanding Causes, Unlocking Solutions*. Washington, DC: United States Institute of Peace Press.

Lievan, Anatol. 2011. *Pakistan: A Hard Country*. New York: Public Affairs.

Lopez, George A. 2008. "Don't Just Do Something: Getting Sanctions Right." *Commonweal*, June 6.

———. 2016. "Mobilizing Sanctions for Preventing Mass Atrocities: From Targeting Dictators to Enablers." In Rosenberg, Galis, and Zucker, *Reconstructing Atrocity Prevention*, 379–92.

Luck, Edward C., and Dana Zaret Luck. 2016. "The Individual Responsibility to Protect." In Rosenberg, Galis, and Zucker, *Reconstructing Atrocity Prevention*, 207–48.

Mach, Katharine J., et al. 2019. "Climate as a Risk Factor for Armed Conflict." *Nature* 571:193–97.

Malinowski, Bronislaw. 2006. "An Anthropological Analysis of War." In *War & Peace in an Age of Terrorism: A Reader*, edited by William M. Evan, 222–26. Boston: Pearson.

Mansfield, Edward D., and Jack Snyder. 2005. *Electing to Fight: Why Emerging Democracies Go to War*. Cambridge, MA: MIT Press.

Marazziti, Mario. 2012. "Lessons in Peace." *America*, November 19.

Martin, James. 2020. "Pope Francis Closes Door on the Death Penalty in 'Fratelli Tutti.'" *America*, October 4.

Massaro, Thomas J., S.J., and Thomas A. Shannon. 2003. *Catholic Perspectives on War and Peace.* Lanham, MD: Rowman & Littlefield.

Mayer, Jane. 2009. *The Dark Side: The Inside Story of How the War on Terror Turned into a War on American Ideals.* New York: Anchor Books.

Mayersen, Deborah. 2016. "Deconstructing Risk and Developing Resilience: The Role of Inhibiting Factors in Genocide Prevention." In Rosenberg, Galis, and Zucker, *Reconstructing Atrocity Prevention,* 277–94.

McCarthy, Eli S., ed. 2020. *A Just Peace Ethic Primer: Building Sustainable Peace and Breaking Cycles of Violence.* Washington, DC: Georgetown University Press.

McFaul, Michael. 2010. *Advancing Democracy Abroad: Why We Should and How We Can.* Lanham, MD: Rowman & Littlefield.

McKeogh, Colm. 2002. *Innocent Civilians: The Morality of Killing in War.* New York: Palgrave.

Mead, Margaret. 2006. "Warfare Is Only an Invention, Not a Biological Necessity." In *War & Peace in an Age of Terrorism: A Reader,* edited by William M. Evan, 218–21. Boston: Pearson.

Megivern, James J. 1997. *The Death Penalty: An Historical and Theological Survey.* New York: Paulist Press.

Mégret, Frédéric. 2009. "Beyond the 'Salvation' Paradigm: Responsibility to Protect (Others) vs the Power of Protecting Oneself." *Security Dialogue* 40 (6): 575–95.

Mehri, Marius, and Paul W. Thurner. 2020. "Military Technology and Human Loss in Interstate Conflict: The Conditional Impact of Arms Imports." *Journal of Conflict Resolution* 64 (6): 1172–96.

Metaxas, Eric. 2007. *Amazing Grace: William Wilberforce and the Heroic Campaign to End Slavery.* New York: HarperCollins.

Mitchell, Sara McLaughlin, and John A. Vasquez, eds. 2021. *What Do We Know about War?* 3rd ed. Lanham, MD: Rowman & Littlefield.

Moorehead, Caroline. 2014. *Village of Secrets: Defying the Nazis in Vichy France.* New York: Harper Perennial.

Morgan, Patrick M. 2006. *International Security: Problems and Solutions.* Washington, DC: CQ Press.

Moyo, Dambisa. 2009. *Dead Aid: Why Aid Is Not Working and How There Is a Better Way for Africa.* New York: Farrar, Straus and Giroux.

Mueller, John. 2004. *The Remnants of War*. Ithaca, NY: Cornell University Press.

Mujica, Barbara. 2011. "Don't Look Away." *Commonweal*, March 25.

Nadelmann, Ethan A. 1990. "Global Prohibition Regimes: The Evolution of Norms in International Society." *International Organization* 44 (4): 479–526.

Neuhaus, Richard John. 2003. "The Sounds of Religion in a Time of War." *First Things*, May.

Newman, Michael. 2009. "Revisiting the 'Responsibility to Protect.'" *Political Quarterly* 80 (1): 92–100.

Norris, John. 2009. *Pistols at Dawn: A History of Dueling*. Gloucestershire: History Press.

O'Connell, Gerard. 2017. "Pope Francis: The Death Penalty Is Contrary to the Gospel." *America*, October 11.

Odendaal, Andries. 2013. *A Crucial Link: Local Peace Communities and National Peacebuilding*. Washington, DC: United States Institute of Peace Press.

Olsen, Tricia D., Leigh A. Payne, and Andrew G. Reiter. 2010. *Transnational Justice in Balance: Comparing Processes, Weighing Efficacy*. Washington, DC: United States Institute of Peace Press.

O'Reilly, Marie. 2015. *Why Women: Inclusive Security and Peaceful Societies*. Washington, DC: Inclusive Security.

Osborn, Ronald. 2011. "Still Counting." *Commonweal*, February 11.

Osnos, Evan. 2017. "On the Brink." *New Yorker*, September 18.

Paffenholz, Thania. 2013. "International Peacebuilding Goes Local: Analysing Lederach's Conflict Transformation Theory and Its Ambivalent Encounter with 20 Years of Practice." *Peacebuilding* 2 (1): 11–27.

Pamp, Oliver, Lukas Rudolph, Paul W. Thurner, Andreas Mehltretter, and Simon Primus. 2018. "The Build-Up of Coercive Capacities: Arms Imports and the Outbreak of Violent Intrastate Conflicts." *Journal of Peace Research* 55 (4): 430–44.

Pape, Robert A. 2006. *Dying to Win: The Strategic Logic of Suicide Bombing*. New York: Random House.

Pape, Robert A., and James K. Feldman. 2010. *Cutting the Fuse: The Explosion of Global Suicide Terrorism & How to Stop It*. Chicago: University of Chicago Press.

Paris, Ronald. 2014. "The 'Responsibility to Protect' and the Structural Problems of Preventative Humanitarian Intervention." *International Peacekeeping* 21 (5): 569–603.

Patterson, Eric. 2007. *Just War Thinking: Morality and Pragmatism in the Struggle against Contemporary Threats*. Lanham, MD: Lexington Books.

Patterson, Orlando. 1982. *Slavery and Social Death: A Comparative Study*. Cambridge, MA: Harvard University Press.

———. 1999. Introduction to *Chronology of World Slavery*, by Junius P. Rodriguez, ix. Santa Barbara, CA: ABC-CLIO.

Pell, Owen, and Kelly Bonner. 2016. "Corporate Behavior and Atrocity Prevention: Is Aiding and Abetting Liability the Best Way to Influence Corporate Behavior?" In Rosenberg, Galis, and Zucker, *Reconstructing Atrocity Prevention*, 393–427.

Peppard, Michael. 2008. "The Secret Weapon: Religious Abuse in the 'War on Terror.'" *Commonweal*, November 30.

Perkoski, Evan, and Erica Chenoweth. 2018. *Nonviolent Resistance and Prevention of Mass Killings during Popular Uprisings*. Washington, DC: International Center on Nonviolent Conflict.

Pinker, Steven. 2011. *The Better Angels of Our Nature: Why Violence Has Declined*. New York: Viking.

———. 2018. *Enlightenment Now: The Case for Reason, Science, Humanism, and Progress*. New York: Viking.

Pinckney, Jonathan. 2018. *When Civil Resistance Succeeds: Building Democracy after Popular Nonviolent Uprisings*. Washington, DC: International Center on Nonviolent Conflict.

Pinkovskiy, Maxim, and Xavier Sala-i-Martin. 2010. "Parametric Estimations of the World Distribution of Income." *Vox*, January 22.

Popovic, Srdja. 2015. *Blueprint for Revolution: How to Use Rice Pudding, Lego Men, and Other Nonviolent Techniques to Galvanize Communities, Overthrow Dictators, or Simply Change the World*. New York: Spiegel & Grau.

Potts, Malcolm, and Thomas Hayden. 2008. *Sex and War: How Biology Explains Warfare and Terrorism and Offers a Path to a Safer World*. Dallas: Benbella Books.

Power, Samantha. 2008. "The Enforcer." *New Yorker*, January 19.

Price, Richard, and Nina Tannenwald. 1996. "Norms and Deterrence: The Nuclear and Chemical Weapons Taboo." In *The Culture of National*

Security: Norms and Identity in World Politics, edited by Peter J. Katzenstein, 114–52. New York: Columbia University Press.

Ramsbotham, Oliver, Tom Woodhouse, and Hugh Miall. 2005. *Contemporary Conflict Resolution: The Prevention, Management and Transformation of Deadly Conflicts*. 2nd ed. Cambridge: Polity Press.

Ratzinger, Joseph. 1998. *Milestones: Memoirs, 1927–1977*. Translated by Erasmo Leiva-Merikakis. San Francisco: Ignatius Press.

Ray, James Lee. 1989. "The Abolition of Slavery and the End of International War." *International Organization* 43 (3): 405–39.

Regan, Patrick M. 2000. *Civil Wars and Foreign Powers: Outside Intervention in Intrastate Conflict*. Ann Arbor: University of Michigan Press.

Repucci, Sarah, and Amy Slipowitz. 2022. *Freedom in the World 2022*. Washington, DC: Freedom House.

Riddell, Roger C. 2007. *Does Foreign Aid Really Work?* Oxford: Oxford University Press.

Ringsmose, Jens. 2008. "When Great Powers Lose Small Wars." *Global Security* 22 (3): 411–18.

Rising, David, and Matt Surman. 2005. "New Pope Made Risky Choices in Bavarian Town during World War II." Associated Press, April 23.

Rosen, Jeffrey. 2008. "Man-Made Disaster." *New Republic*, December 24.

Rosenbaum, Ron. 2010. "Ban Drone-Porn War Crimes." *Slate*, August 31.

Rosenberg, Sheri R., Tibi Galis, and Alex Zucker, eds. 2016. *Reconstructing Atrocity Prevention*. Cambridge: Cambridge University Press.

Roser, Max, Joe Hasell, Bastian Herre, and Bobbie Macdonald. 2016. "War and Peace." Our World in Data. https://ourworldindata.org/war-and-peace.

Roth, Richard. 2009. *American Homicide*. Cambridge, MA: Harvard University Press.

Rubin, Barnett R. 2008. "The Politics of Security in Postconflict Statebuilding." In Call and Wyeth, *Building States to Build Peace*, 25–47.

Rummel, R. J. 1997. *Power Kills: Democracy as a Method of Nonviolence*. New Brunswick, NJ: Transaction Publishers.

Russett, Bruce. 1993. *Grasping the Democratic Peace: Principles for a Post–Cold War World*. Princeton: Princeton University Press.

———. 2008. "Advance Democracy, Human Rights, and Interdependence." In Stassen, *Just Peacemaking*, 116–31.

Russett, Bruce, and John Oneal. 2001. *Triangulating Peace: Democracy, Interdependence, and International Organizations*. New York: W.W. Norton.

Sachs, Jeffrey D. 2005. *The End of Poverty: Economic Possibilities for Our Time*. New York: Penguin.

Sageman, Marc. 2008. *Leaderless Jihad: Terror Networks in the Twenty-First Century*. Philadelphia: University of Pennsylvania Press.

Saiya, Nilay. 2021. "Why Freedom Defeats Terrorism." *Journal of Democracy* 32 (2): 105–15.

Sample, Susan G. 2002. "The Outcomes of Military Buildups: Minor States v. Major Powers." *Journal of Peace Research* 39 (6): 669–91.

Sampson, Cynthia. 2007. "Religion and Peacebuilding." In Zartman, *Peacemaking in International Conflict*, 273–323.

Scahill, Jeremy. 2008. *Blackwater: The Rise of the World's Most Powerful Army*. Rev. ed. New York: Nation Books.

Schall, James V. 2004. "When War Must Be the Answer." *Policy Review*, no. 128 (December/January): 59–70.

Schell, Jonathan. 2003. *The Unconquerable World: Power, Nonviolence, and the Will of the People*. New York: Holt.

Sémelin, Jacques, Claire Andrieu, and Sarah Gensburger. 2014. *Resisting Genocide: The Multiple Forms of Rescue*. Oxford: Oxford University Press.

Senese, Paul D., and John A. Vasquez. 2005. "Assessing the Steps to War." *British Journal of Political Science* 35 (4): 607–33.

Seybolt, Taylor B. 2007. *Humanitarian Military Intervention: The Conditions for Success and Failure*. Oxford: Oxford University Press.

Shadle, Matthew A. 2011. *The Origins of War: A Catholic Perspective*. Washington, DC: Georgetown University Press.

Sharp, Gene. 1990a. *Civilian-Based Defense: A Post-Military Weapons System*. Princeton: Princeton University Press.

———. 1990b. "Nonviolent Action: An Active Technique of Struggle." In *Nonviolence in Theory and Practice*, edited by Robert L. Holmes, 147–50. Belmont, CA: Wadsworth.

———. 2005. *Waging Nonviolent Struggle: 20th Century Practice and 21st Century Potential*. Boston: Extending Horizons Books.

Sharp, Gene, and Bruce Jenkins. 2003. *The Anti-Coup*. Boston: Albert Einstein Institute.

Shaw, Martin. 2003. *War and Genocide*. Cambridge: Polity.

Sheehan, James J. 2008. *Where Have All the Soldiers Gone? The Transformation of Modern Europe*. Boston: Mariner Books.

Shue, Henry. 2010. "Targeting Civilian Infrastructure with Smart Bombs: The New Permissiveness." *Philosophy & Public Policy Quarterly* 30 (3/4): 2–8.

Slim, Hugo. 2008. *Killing Civilians: Method, Madness, and Morality in War*. New York: Columbia University Press.

Snyder, Timothy. 2010. *Bloodlands: Europe between Hitler and Stalin*. New York: Basic Books.

———. 2015. *Black Earth: The Holocaust as History and Warning*. New York: Penguin Random House.

Sørensen, Georg. 2008. *Democracy and Democratization: Processes and Prospects in a Changing World*. 3rd ed. Boulder, CO: Westview Press.

Sparks, Justin, John Follain, and Christopher Morgan. 2005. "Papal Hopeful Is a Former Hitler Youth." *Sunday Times* (London), April 17.

Spierenburg, Pieter. 2008. *A History of Murder: Personal Violence in Europe from the Middle Ages to the Present*. Cambridge: Polity.

Stassen, Glen H., ed. 2008. *Just Peacemaking: The New Paradigm for the Ethics of Peace and War*. New ed. Cleveland: Pilgrim Press.

Stephan, Maria J. 2020. "Making Just Peace Possible." In McCarthy, *Just Peace Ethic Primer*, 143–56.

Stephan, Maria, and Erica Chenoweth. 2008. "Why Civil Resistance Works: The Strategic Logic of Nonviolent Conflict. *International Security* 33 (1): 7–44.

Stephan, Maria J., Sadaf Lakhani, and Nadia Naviwala. 2015. *Aid to Civil Society: A Movement Mindset*. Washington, DC: United States Institute of Peace Press.

Stewart, Frances. 2002. "Root Causes of Violent Conflict in Developing Countries." *British Medical Journal* 324:342–45.

Stoessinger, John G. 2005. *Why Nations Go to War*. 9th ed. Belmont, CA: Wadsworth.

Straus, Scott. 2012. "'Destroy Them to Save Us': Theories of Genocide and the Logics of Political Violence." *Terrorism and Political Violence* 24 (4): 544–60.

Thomsen, Michael. 2011. "Shooting Gallery." *Slate*, September 12.

Tirman, John. 2011. *The Deaths of Others: The Fate of Civilians in America's Wars.* Oxford: Oxford University Press.

Toulmin, Stephen. 1992. "The Limits of Allegiance in a Nuclear Age." In *Just War Theory*, edited by Jean Bethke Elshtain, 280–98. New York: New York University Press.

Twilley, Nicola. 2022. "The Cold Rush." *New Yorker*, August 22.

United Nations Development Programme. *Human Development Index.* Human Development Reports. United Nations. https://hdr.undp.org/data-center/human-development-index#/indicies/HDI.

Uppsala Conflict Data Program website. Department of Peace and Conflict Research, Uppsala University. https://ucdp.uu.se/.

Uvin, Peter. 2004. *Human Rights and Development.* Bloomfield, CT: Kumarian.

Valentino, Benjamin. 2004. *Final Solutions: Mass Killings and Genocide in the 20th Century.* Ithaca, NY: Cornell University Press.

Varshney, Ashutosh. 2002. *Ethnic Conflict and Civic Life: Hindus and Muslims in India.* New Haven: Yale University Press.

Vassilev, Rossen. 2010. "The Rescue of Bulgaria's Jews in World War II." *New Politics* 12 (4): 114–21.

Waldrep, Christopher. 2002. *The Many Faces of Judge Lynch: Extralegal Violence and Punishment in America.* New York: Palgrave Macmillan.

Wallensteen, Peter. 2007. *Understanding Conflict Resolution: War, Peace and the Global System.* 2nd ed. Los Angeles: SAGE.

Walsh, Declan. 2021. "Where Did Chad Rebels Prepare for Their Own War? In Libya." *New York Times*, April 22.

Walzer, Michael. 1992. *Just and Unjust Wars.* 2nd ed. New York: Basic Books.

Ward, Michael D., and Kristian S. Gleditsch. 1998. "Democratizing for Peace." *American Political Science Review* 92 (1): 51–61.

Weaver, James H., Michael T. Rock, and Kenneth Kusterer. 1997. *Achieving Broad-Based Sustainable Development: Governance, Environment, and Growth with Equity.* West Hartford, CT: Kumarian Press.

Weigand, Krista E., and Emilia Justyna Powell. 2011. "Past Experience, Quest for the Best Forum, and Peaceful Attempts to Resolve Territorial Disputes." *Journal of Conflict Resolution* 55 (1): 33–59.

Weigel, George. 2003. "Moral Clarity in a Time of War." *First Things*, January.

———. 2010. "Through a Glass, Clearly." *First Things*, August/September.
Weil, Simone. 1977. "*The Iliad*, Poem of Might." In *The Simone Weil Reader*, edited by George A. Panichas, 153–83. New York: David McKay Company.
Welsh, Jennifer M. 2016. "The 'Narrow but Deep Approach' to Implementing the Responsibility to Protect: Reassessing the Focus on International Crimes." In Rosenberg, Galis, and Zucker, *Reconstructing Atrocity Prevention*, 81–94.
Welzer, Harald. 2017. *Climate Wars: Why People Will Be Killed in the 21st Century*. Translated by Patrick Camiller. Cambridge: Polity.
Wendt, Alexander. 1992. "Anarchy Is What States Make of It: The Social Construction of Power Politics." *International Organization* 46 (2): 391–425.
———. 1999. *Social Theory of International Politics*. Cambridge: Cambridge University Press.
Whitlock, Craig. 2010. "Members of U.S. Platoon in Afghanistan Accused of Killing Civilians for Sport." *Washington Post*, September 18.
Wilcock, Evelyn. 2012. "Impossible Pacifism: Jews, the Holocaust, and Nonviolence." In *Nonviolence in Theory and Practice*, 3rd ed., edited by Robert L. Holmes and Barry L. Gan, 194–204. Long Grove, IL: Waveland Press.
Winright, Tobias. 2007. "Community Policing as a Paradigm for International Relations." In *Just Policing, Not War: An Alternative Response to World Violence*, edited by Gerald W. Schlabach, 130–52. Collegeville, MN: Liturgical Press.
———. 2011. "Predictably Horrific." *Commonweal*, March 25.
———. 2015. "The (Im)Morality of Cluster Munitions." In *Can War Be Just in the 21st Century? Ethicists Engage the Tradition*, edited by Tobias Winright and Laurie Johnston, 29–49. Maryknoll, NY: Orbis Books.
Wittes, Tamara Cofman. 2008. *Freedom's Unsteady March: America's Role in Building Arab Democracy*. Washington, DC: Brookings Institution Press.
Wright, Lawrence. 2006. *The Looming Tower: Al-Qaeda and the Road to 9/11*. New York: Vintage Books.
Yoder, John Howard. 1992. *Nevertheless: The Varieties and Shortcomings of Religious Pacifism*. Rev. ed. Scottdale, PA: Herald Press.

Zakaria, Fareed. 2007. *The Future of Freedom: Illiberal Democracy at Home and Abroad.* New ed. New York: Norton.

Zartman, I. William. *Peacemaking in International Conflict: Methods & Techniques.* Rev. ed. Washington, DC: United States Institute of Peace Press.

Zunes, Stephen. 2017. *Civil Resistance against Coups: A Comparative and Historical Perspective.* Washington, DC: International Center on Nonviolent Conflict.

INDEX

A
"Achilles heel of all governments," 42–43
"active nonviolence," 31
Ad Beattissimi Apostolorum (Benedict XV), 7
Albright, George Washington, 112
alternatives, to war, 56–57
Anderson, Mary, 49
arbitration, conflict, 66–67
Aristotle, on slavery, 112
armed conflict
    international law reduction of, 62–65
    stop-and-start cycle, 69–72, 98–99
    trends in, 121–22
armed force, track record of, 39–40
arms control, treaties, 61–62
arms trade, 30
"asymmetrical warfare," 60–61
Augustine, on slavery, 112

B
Bacevich, Andrew, 33
Bae, Sangmin, 108
Bancroft, Edward, 112
Bartlett, Robert, 109
battleproofing, soldiers, 24
"below the military horizon," 107
Benedict XV (pope), 7
    on impacts of war, 10
Benedict XVI (pope)
    on active nonviolence, 31
    as POW, 18–19
Blattman, Christopher, 36
Bourke, Joanna, 12
Boutros, Victor, 97

C
capital punishment, justification of, 107–8
capital punishment, progress without perfection example, 105
Caritas in Veritate (Benedict XVI), 53, 78
carnivalesque, the, 24
Carvalho, Manuel, 33
Centesimus Annus (John Paul II), 27, 30–31, 77, 81, 101, 102–3
chattel slavery. *see* enslaved peoples
Chenoweth, Erica, 39, 43–44
children, war's impacts on, 9–10
Civil Resistance (Chenoweth), 44

178 Index

civil resistance, nonviolent, 42–50
civil society, vibrancy of, as war risk factor, 95
civil wars
   lowering risks of, 94
   resolutions of, 69–72
civilians, deaths of innocent, 13–17
combatants, deaths of, 18–19
conflict prevention and resolution, 66–67
"consociationalism," 94
corruption, fighting, 96–97
Cortright, David, 82
coverups, in war, 32–34
"curse, resource," 83, 87

D
death penalty
   abolishment of, 113–18
   normalization of, 107–8
   progress without perfection example, 105
deaths, wartime, 13–17, 18–19
debt collecting, starting a war for, 57
debt relief, foreign aid in, 89–90
dehumanization conditioning, 23–26
democratic governments
   peaceful effects of, 90–98
   worldwide trends in, 123
"democratic peace, the," 91–92
disarmament, 56
Douglas, Mary, 118
dueling
   abolishment of, 115
   normalization of, 110–11

E
economic conditions, as risk of war, 83, 85–90
economic development, creating peace with, 78–82
effectiveness, of war, 27–29
enslaved peoples
   abolishment of, 115–18
   normalization of, 111–13
environment, war's effects on, 79–80, 84, 90
equality, gender, in government, 95
Evangelii Nuntiandi (Paul VI), 76
Evangelium Vitae (John Paul II), 79
expectations and norms, of countries, 57–58

F
failures, of wars, 36–42
families, war's impacts on, 9–10
Finnemore, Martha, 57–58
Fitzhugh, George, 112
foreign aid, for building peace, 88–90
Francis (pope), 3, 9, 66
   on nonviolence, 30
   on ravages of war, 9
Fratelli Tutti (Francis), 10, 27–28, 56
Fry, Douglas, 107

G
Gaudium et Spes, 75, 101
gender inequality
   in government, 95
   as war risk factor, 83, 87–88

genocide, during resistance movements, 47–48, 50
Getting Better (Kenny), 122
Giugale, Marcelo, 85
global common good, 76
global health initiatives, as foreign aid, 90
globalization, collaboration through, 51–56, 57–60
Goering, Hermann, 33
good, global common, 76
Governance for Peace (Cortright, Seyle, and Wall), 82–83
governments, democratic, peaceful effects of, 90–98
gray-area killings, 15
Grossman, Dave, 12, 24

H
Hackworth, David, 25
Hathaway, Oona, 62
Haugen, Gary, 97
health initiatives, global, as foreign aid, 90
Hedges, Chris, 31–32
History of Warfare, A (Keegan), 120
How Enemies Become Friends (Kupchan), 66
How Terrorist Groups End (Jones and Libicki), 61
Human Development Index, UN, 122
human trait, warfare as a, 106–7
humanitarian interventions, armed, 40–42, 48

I
Iliad essay (Weil), 25
inequality, group, as war risk factor, 83
innocent victims, deaths of, 13–17
institutional violence
  abolishment of, 113–18
  normalization of, 107–13
international law
  armed conflict reduction with, 62–65
  importance of, 54–55
Internationalists (Hathaway and Shapiro), 62–65
interventions
  aftermath of, 46–47
  armed humanitarian, 40–42, 48
  genocide during, 47–48, 50
  unarmed, 42–50
invention, of war, 106–7

J
John Paul II (pope), 27, 30–31, 79, 81, 101–2
John XXIII (pope), 53
Jones, Seth, 61
just and peaceful world, envisioning a, 76–77
just order, 8–9

K
Kaplan, Oliver, 49
Keegan, John, 107, 120
Kellogg-Briand Pact (1928), 63–65
Kenny, Charles, 122
Khatam, Hanzera, 22

Kiernan, V.G., 110–11
killing at scale, 12–13
killings, gray-area, 15
Krasniqi-Goodman, Vasfije, 22
Kupchan, Charles, 66

L
Lamb, Christina, 21
law enforcement, transnational, 61
Levinger, Matthew, 66
Libicki, Martin, 61
Libya, military intervention in, 41–42
Locust Effect, The (Haugen and Boutros), 97–98
"lootable resources," 83

M
mass atrocities, warning signs of, 73
Mead, Margaret, 106–7
mediation, conflict, 66–67
militarism, 33–35
military power, success and, 38
military spending, economic growth and, 85, 86
Mueller, John, 96, 119–20
Mukunizwa, Jane, 22

N
"naive realism," 36
Narcisa Claveria, Lola, 22
New American Militarism, The (Bacevich), 33–35
noncombatants, deaths of, 13–17
"nonviolence, active," 31
norms and expectations, of countries, 57–58, 65–66

O
"obligation to assist" principle, 48–49
Octogesima Adveniens (Paul VI), 82
On Killing (Grossman), 24
Opting Out of War (Anderson), 49
order, tranquility of, 8
Our Bodies, Their Battlefields (Lamb), 21–23
"outcasting," 65

P
Pacem in Terris (John XXIII), 53
Paris Peace Pact (1928), 63–65
Patterson, Orlando, 111
Paul VI (pope), 76, 82
"peace, the democratic," 91–92
peace, understanding, 75–82, 90–98
peaceful alternatives, to war, 56–57
peacekeepers, third-party, 69–72
perfection, progress without, 102, 103–5
political factors, in peace building, 90–98
political injustice, as threat to peace, 80–81
Postlethwayt, Malachy, 112
presidential representation systems, 94
prevention, war, 60–68
prevention and resolution, conflict, 66–67
progress, global, trends in, 122
progress without perfection, 102, 103–5

R

rape, as weapon of war, 21–23
"realism, naive," 36
Remnants of War, The (Mueller), 119–20
resistance movements
   genocide during, 47–48, 50
   unarmed, 42–50
Resisting War (Kaplan), 49
"resource curse," 83, 87
"resources, lootable," 83
responsibility-to-protect principle, 40, 41, 48
risks of war
   economic conditions as, 85–90
   overview of, 83–84
   political factors, 90–98

S

Second Vatican Council, in the global common good, 76
security force defection, 43, 45
Seybolt, Taylor, 41
Seyle, Conor, 82
Shapiro, Scott, 62
Sharp, Gene, 42
sin, structural, 102–4
slavery, chattel. *See* enslaved peoples
Slavery and Social Death (Patterson), 111–12
social factors, as war risk factor, 83–84, 86
social institutions, normalizing institutional violence, 118–19
soldiers, deaths of, 18–19
solidarity, virtue of, 77

Sollicitudo rei Socialis (John Paul II), 77
Stephan, Maria, 43–44
stop-and-start armed conflict cycle, 69–72, 98–99
structural sin, 102–4
successes, of wars, 36–42

T

terrorism, tactics, 60–61
Tirman, John, 33
tranquility of order, 8
transnational law enforcement, 61
transparency, government, 97
trial by ordeal or combat, 109–10, 114–15

U

unarmed resistance movements, 42–50
United Nations, 55, 122
universal common good, 52

V

violence, institutional
   abolishment of, 113–18
   normalization of, 107–13

W

Wall, Kristen, 82
Wallensteen, Peter, 94
War Is a Force That Gives Us Meaning (Hedge), 31–32
"War Is Only an Invention— Not a Biological Necessity" (Mead), 106–7

"warfare, asymmetrical," 60–61
warfare, origins of, 106–7
Weil, Simone, 25
Wendt, Alexander, 57–58
Why Civil Resistance Works (Chenoweth and Stephan), 43–44
Why We Fight (Blattman), 36–37
Wilson, John Lyde, 111
World Day of Peace Message, 2000 (John Paul II), 29, 123
World Day of Peace Message, 2017 (Benedict XVI), 31
World Day of Peace Message, 2021 (Francis), 9
World Synod of Catholic Bishops (1971) on economic development, 81–82

DAVID CARROLL COCHRAN is professor of politics and co-director of the peace and justice minor at Loras College. He is the author or editor of five previous books, most recently *The Catholic Church in Ireland Today* and *Catholic Realism and the Abolition of War*.

www.ingramcontent.com/pod-product-compliance
Lightning Source LLC
Chambersburg PA
CBHW061940220426
43662CB00012B/1980